The Closing Chapters of Long Lives: Results from the 10-Year Swilsoo Study on the Oldest Old

THE CLOSING CHAPTERS OF LONG LIVES: RESULTS FROM THE 10-YEAR SWILSOO STUDY ON THE OLDEST OLD

EDITH GUILLEY
CHRISTIAN J. LALIVE D'EPINAY
AND ASSOCIATES
EDITORS

ENGLISH EDITING BY IAN HAMILTON

Nova Science Publishers, Inc.
New York

For permission to use material from this book please contact us:
Telephone 631-231-7269; Fax 631-231-8175
Web Site: http://www.novapublishers.com

LIBRARY OF CONGRESS CATALOGING-IN-PUBLICATION DATA

The closing chapters of long lives : results from the 10-year Swilsoo study on the oldest old / [edited by] Edith Guilley and Christian J. Lalive d'Epinay.

p. cm.

ISBN 978-1-60456-971-1 (hardcover)

1. Older people--Longitudinal studies. 2. Aging--Psychological aspects--Longitudinal studies. I. Guilley, Edith. II. Lalive d'Epinay, Christian.

HQ1061.C556 2008

155.67--dc22 2008027822

Published by Nova Science Publishers, Inc. New York

CONTENTS

PREFACE

One of the most striking demographic changes over the last century in Western countries has been the rapid growth, both absolute and relative, of the oldest-old population, to such an extent that living beyond the age of 80 years constitutes a new stage of life.

But what is life like after 80? Rather than scrutinizing the pathologies of very old age, this book enquires into the normal aging of the oldest old, their health trajectories, their socio-demographic inequalities; it analyzes their daily life, including their social relationships, social support, and activities, and observes how the oldest old adapt to the multiple stresses and challenges of very old age. The book reports major results obtained from Swilsoo, a long-term longitudinal study based on two cohorts of octogenarians. The two cohorts were assessed on an approximately yearly basis, the first for 9 waves from 1994 to 2004, with 340 participants at inception, and the second for 5 waves from 1999 to 2004, initially with 377 participants.

This book demonstrates that many common stereotypes concerning the oldest old are false. For examples, their main shared characteristic is not sickness, but frailty, which affects them in different ways. A long life does not necessarily culminate in dependence. Dependence is a risk--especially among persons of lower socio-economic status--but not an ineluctable outcome. It also helps to bring out the importance of social and psychological resources in the lives of the oldest old. Although multiple stresses such as negative health-related changes or self-reported bereavements of a loved one often occur in the life of the elderly and affect their health and well-being, the very old can take advantage of various resources or adjustment mechanisms to help preserve their well-being and robustness. The book shows for instance that the preservation by the elderly of a positive and active role within the family is a boon to their health and that the continuation of leisure activities or the effective use of psychological resources counters the negative effects of frailty on well-being.

In: The Closing Chapters of Long Lives
Editors: E. Guilley, Ch. J. Lalive d'Epinay

ISBN: 978-1-60456-971-1

Introduction: The Closing Chapters of Long Lives - A Presentation

This book focuses on the life and health trajectories of the very old, on the environmental, social and psychological factors that shape these trajectories, on the impact the latter have on elders' everyday life and the way in which the very old cope with the events that punctuate their lives. In so doing, it presents results obtained from the Swiss Interdisciplinary Longitudinal Study on the Oldest Old (Swilsoo), a research program which followed two successive birth cohorts of octogenarians, one formed between 1910 and 1914 and monitored over a period of 10 years (1994-2004), and the other formed between 1915 and 1920 and monitored over a period of five years (1999-2004).

The Rise of the Oldest Old

To live beyond 80? For thousands of years, this feat seemed to be the preserve of such exceptional individuals as Plato or the Buddha. True, demographers have established that in ancient times around 4 to 5 percent of children born reached this ripe old age (Dupâquier & Dupâquier, 1985), implying that the feat was not so rare, but people generally saw it as something unusual. Moreover, this view was supported by the Bible, our civilisation's authoritative source: "Seventy is the sum of our years, or eighty if we are strong" (Psalm 90, v 10).

What was still true up to about 1900 underwent a profound change in the century that followed. In 1900, in Western countries as a whole, anyone reaching or going beyond this canonical age was indeed a survivor of his or her birth cohort. In Switzerland, for example, of 100 men born before 1820 only eight were to become octogenarians, and of 100 women, nine. Compare that with the Swilsoo cohort formed between 1910 and 1914, where four women out of ten and one man in four were to pass this milestone (Office Fédéral de la Statistique, 1996). In one century, life expectancy soared by about two thirds and, for those entering adulthood today it is reasonable to predict that, barring accidents, they will be able to experience life beyond 80.

A logical outcome of this astonishing increase in life expectancy has been a surge in the number of very old persons, who now constitute the fastest growing age class. Between 1900 and 2000, the total population of the United States was multiplied by 3.6 and that of persons aged 80 or over by 24! In Canada, the equivalent multipliers were 5.5 for total population and 25 for the very old ; in Switzerland, while the total population barely doubled, the number of over-eighties climbed from 17,000 to 300,000!

THE OLDEST OLD: A NEW FIELD OF RESEARCH

While advanced old age has now acquired the status of statistical normality and seems to impose itself upon us with the force of destiny, what do we know of this final stage of life? To be honest, not much. Spurred by demographers' warnings about the changing age structure of populations, gerontology, involving the multidisciplinary study of ageing and older people, has been developing since the 1950's but was slow in recognizing that growing longevity brings with it new ages of life and a need to differentiate between distinct ages within old age. Constricted by a conventional definition setting the threshold of old age at 60 to 65 years, researchers worked on samples that glossed over the specificity of older people because of their minor importance in statistics ; the average portait of a so-called elderly person in epidemiological surveys of the time was that of a person approaching the age of 70.

Yet as far back as 1974, in the course of a lecture given to the *American Academy of Political and Social Sciences*, Bernice Neugarten proposed making a distinction between the *old old* and persons in the 65-74 age bracket, whom she christened the *young old*. In her view, from the demographic and epidemiological standpoints, the age of 75 was the true brink of old age (Neugarten, 1974). Ten years later, in 1984, the *American Association for the Advancement of Science* requested Matilda Riley and Richard Suzman to organise its annual conference on the theme of the *oldest old,* a term specially coined for the occasion to designate those who manage to pierce the 85-year age barrier. As the authors themselves admit, the choice of that particular age was an arbitrary one, and the first publication to emerge from the conference was described as exploratory : « Because of the current lack of precise information about this population, these papers represent work in progress » (Richard M. Suzman & Riley, 1985). Seven years later, under a title retaining the term *oldest old*, a second publication appeared, this time directed by Richard Suzman, David Willis and Kenneth Manton, and consisting of revised articles from the 1985 work together with some new chapters (Richard M. Suzman, Willis, & Manton, 1992).

It was thus in the second half of the 1980's that the need to recognise the specificity of the very old, of the elderly in the true sense, became apparent. In 1985, the *National Institute of Aging* (*NIA*) launched the first research program to deal specifically with the subject of the *oldest old*. The publications of 1985 and 1992 not only designated the *oldest old* as a new topic for scientific attention ; they also marked out the research field and set forth the program. In the 1992 book, the section entitled « The dynamics of becoming the oldest old » is divided into four parts: disability and mortality, epidemiology of disability, the impact of Alzheimer's disease and, as a corollary to these afflictions, the use of institutional long-term care. In essence, unlike the other ages of life that as a rule are presented in terms of their potential, advanced old age as a focus of scientific investigation is conceived in terms of its pathologies, morbidities and mortality. Is advanced old age merely a pathological age?

Once the momentum had been created, various research projects came into being throughout the world. In 1992/1993, when Swilsoo was designed, there were still few longitudinal studies devoted specifically to the oldest old (Hofer & Piccinin, 2007). Among the most representative ones[1], there were the five following studies : the Cambridge City over 75 Cohort Study aimed at assessing the dementia prevalence (O'Connor et al., 1989); the *Kungsholmen Project* examined the dementia risk factors of persons aged over 75 in the region around Stockholm (Small, Basun, & Bäckman, 1998); the *Lund 80+ Study*, again Swedish, constituted an interdisciplinary approach to the ageing process centered on its physiological, biological and psychological components, and on the needs for care (Svensson, Dehlin, Hagberg, & Samuelsson, 1993); the *Nuns Study* has, since 1986, been analysing the physiological and psychological effects of ageing, particularly of Alzheimer's disease, among a group of nuns aged 75 to 103 (Snowdon, Kemper, & Mortimer, 1999); lastly, the *Octogenarian Twin Study* has target twins in order to elucidate the interaction of biological and environmental factors in ageing (McClearn et al., 1997).

It is clear from the above that, with the possible exception of the last-mentioned study, which would come under the heading of fundamental research, the other four remain true to the program set out in the 1992 publication in that they focus on the pathologies of ageing and the needs for care. Where do we stand with regard to studies dealing more generally with life in advanced old age, how daily life is organised, the forms of support and exchanges within the family, relations with friends, intellectual and spiritual life, and the feeling of well-being? Up to the beginning of Swilsoo, such topics had received relatively scant attention and the literature had little to say about the very old and their life-worlds[2]. Let us consider for a moment two longitudinal studies that in part share the aims of our own work. The first was carried out by a doctor who had received some training in sociology. After taking up a medical post in the Norwegian port of Larvik, T. Romoren decided in 1980 to follow the fortunes of all the persons aged over 80 in Larvik. At that time they were 434 in number; the last of them died in 1999 at the age of 99. That event triggered the start of the study, which took the form of a retrospective longitudinal analysis of the death of each person back to 1980. Romoren had at his disposal the medical records of all his subjects and information on their institutional history (home care, periods of residence in specialised establishments, etc.). In addition, when each person died he interviewed the deceased's principal caregiver. The analysis enabled Romoren to trace with precision the elders' health trajectories and the use they had made of formal medical and institutional services, taking into account the circle of close friends and family around them and the informal support they enjoyed (Romoren, 2003; Romoren & Blekeseaune, 2003).

The study has its limitations, particularly the fact, as the author neatly points out, that the elders themselves are voiceless; we know nothing of their daily life, of the part they played in regulating the events that affected them, of their perception of the care provided, of their experience of long-term care establishments and, more generally, of their reaction to

---

[1] Based on population and not on volunteers

[2] Worthy of mention here is the pioneering study by Bury and Holme (1991), "Life after Ninety ", which, while not based on longitudinal data, was the fruit of in-depth interviews.

advancing age and the approach of death. None the less, the study makes a unique contribution to knowledge of the last years of life.

In San Francisco, Colleen Johnson and Barbara Barer (1997) responded to the call made in 1985 by the NIA in the context of its first program on the *oldest old* by devising a study aimed at identifying the resources and capacities that enable people to carry on living at home, in an urban environment, at an age when the body's inadequacies are ever more keenly felt, while at the same time preserving a genuine feeling of well-being. The objective was thus « to explore the objective and subjective experiences of daily life, and those capacities needed to manage both the physical and social environments and sustain a sense of well-being » (Johnson & Barer, 1997, p3). The methodology chosen was basically to take an anthropological approach with the emphasis on in-depth interviews and to adopt a six-year longitudinal design, with interviews every 14 to 16 months. The qualitative work was accompanied by a standardised questionnaire intended to collect information mainly on health status, social and family resources, and psychological faculties. The sample consisted initially of 150 persons aged over 85 living in San Francisco; by the end of the six-year span, this number had dwindled to 48. The book is an anthropological invitation to share in the life of the elders, with all its challenges. In addition to its wealth of descriptions and its finely shaded presentation of cases and of individual trajectories, the study formulates some general ideas concerning the specificity of advanced old age, ideas that offer some promising avenues for further research. Two in particular are noteworthy. One concerns a reappraisal of the notion of disengagement; activity and social participation may be relevant for the *young old* but the increasing frailty inherent in very old age, with the onset and aggravation of various disabilities, obliges elders to reconsider their social and other engagements and to make a series of major adjustments to their daily life. The preservation of well-being calls for various forms of withdrawal, not only practical but also relational or affective. The other questions the notion that successful ageing depends on the preservation and continuity of self. On the contrary, the authors assert, as elders become increasingly drawn into the world of survivors and are obliged to negotiate the many-faceted losses entailed, they are compelled to revise drastically their self-image, their relations with others, and their conception of time, of life as well as of death. The paradoxical finding that older people are able to face up to a life burdened with more and more losses and yet at the same time retain a genuine feeling of well-being leads the authors to sense a characteristic aura among survivors – hence their book's subtitle, *The aura of survivorship* – the aura being something like a new dimension of their identity born of the fact that they go on living well beyond their assigned life span.

Swilsoo and "The Closing Chapters of Long Lives"

The Swiss Interdisciplinary Longitudinal Study on the Oldest Old (Swilsoo) was designed to enquire into life and health trajectories in advanced old age and their repercussions on the ordering of everyday life. The initial premise was not one of a pathological population but rather one of a population made up, even in very old age, of persons in widely differing states of health but all faced with the prospect that their health would fail gradually in the coming years. In his now definitive work, E. H. Erikson described the challenge of old age as a conflict between despair and integrity (Erikson, 1982). How can the constraints that old age inexorably brings to bear on a person's physical and psychological integrity be confronted without lapsing into despair? As we would put it, the challenge is to preserve one's autonomy in negotiating the limitations imposed by growing frailty. Our project, like Romoren's, seeks to define the architecture of advanced old age, with its principal health trajectories. But we endeavor at the same time to clarify the implications of such ageing on everyday life and the successive restructurings it must undergo, on events and on the way they are regulated. In that sense, our aims coincide with those of Johnson and Barer, with the difference that the latter's qualitative study, based on a limited sample, was « exploratory » in nature whereas our research was based on a sample five times larger (see chapter 1), enabling us to apply essentially quantitative methods of analysis.

The Closing Chapters of Long Lives: A Presentation

The book starts with an introductory chapter which has a twofold purpose : (i) to describe the research project, its methodological choices and its design, and to recapitulate the progress of 10 years of field research, (ii) to familiarise readers with the respondents, the 717 members of the two samples studied, by outlining their collective biography and portraying roughly their sociodemographic, familial and health situation at the time the project started, when they were aged between 80 and 84.

Following this, the book is divided into four parts, each consisting of two chapters. *Architecture of very old age: patterns of health trajectories.* The first part deals with the principal health states in advanced old age. In chapter 2, we dwell upon the notion of frailty and show that frailty is the dominant health status in the oldest old population. We go on to describe the main health transitions and the probability of their occurrence. Chapter 3 questions the assertion that a long life inevitably culminates in a period of long-term dependence. We show that, while long-term dependence is a real possibility – one which varies, moreover, according to gender and social status – it is a risk rather than a shared destiny.

Events and changes: In the second part, we examine how events and changes affect life in advanced old age. Chapter 4 focuses on older people's perception of such events and changes and contains a suggested classification of events in order to identify their consequences. A particularly painful disruption, the death of a loved one, is the subject of chapter 5. We look at the way death takes its toll on family and friends, transforming elders into survivors. We look also at the elders' attitude towards death and at the effects on their health and well-being of losing close ones.

Social networks and relationships of the elders: The third part is devoted to social relationships in very old age. We see elders not as mere recipients of support from the family but more as participants in an exchange. Our data show that, even in conditions of growing frailty and with more frequent support from close ones, many of the very old endeavour to maintain the principle of reciprocity in exchanges and to keep playing an active role in the family (chapter 6). It seems also that this stance is of benefit to the elders' health, boosting their ability to remain robust (chapter 7). In chapter 8, the interface between formal and informal support is under scrutiny; according to the results, the concern that the introduction of formal services may curb the responsibilities of close relatives is, with few exception, unfunded.

Preserving well-being: The question of well-being is taken up in the fourth part, where we develop two main themes. First, in chapter 9, we examine the relationship between the activities of daily life and well-being, concluding that those who, despite declining health, manage to keep up certain activities preserve in this way their well-being. In chapter 10, we turn the spotlight on to the effectiveness of one particular coping mechanism. It appears that downward social comparison (i.e. comparing one's own situation with that of others who are worse off) makes it easier to cope with one's own frailty and maintain well-being.

A Team Effort

This book is the outcome of a team effort led by Christian Lalive d'Epinay (Swilsoo's principal investigator) and Edith Guilley (Swilsoo's associate director from 2003 to 2008). The contributors are all active in various fields of research and have been associated for many years with the work of the Center for Interdisciplinary Gerontology (CIG ; see list of contributors). The overall structure of the book was agreed upon in common and responsibility for the preparation and drafting of each chapter was entrusted to a team selected in light of each member's special interests and qualifications, but the successive versions of each chapter were the subject of general discussions.

Three other persons made substantial contributions, namely: Christian Cordonier, who directed the survey work up to 2002 and constructed the database; Tatiana Nagovsky, CIG documentalist, who fulfilled our literature requests with boundless patience; and Ian Hamilton, who shouldered the difficult task of editing our texts or translating them into English.

Our thanks also go to the members of the Scientific Council (see below) for their remarks, suggestions and encouragement over the years.

Lastly, we warmly acknowledge the invaluable contribution of the 717 octogenarians who agreed to be witnesses of the human condition in advanced old age.

Institutional Framework

The Swiss Interdisciplinary Longitudinal Study on the Oldest Old (Swilsoo) was a project of the Center for Interdisciplinary Gerontology of the University of Geneva, carried out under the direction of Prof. Christian Lalive d'Epinay (sociologist, principal investigator to the Swiss National Science Foundation (SNF)), and a scientific committee composed of professors Anik de Ribaupierre (developmental psychologist), Jean-Pierre Michel (geriatrician), Gabrielle Antille (econometrician), Alain Clémence (social psychologist), Hermann-Michel Hagmann (demographer), Eugène Horber (methodologist), Charles-Henri Rapin (geriatrician) and Dario Spini (social psychologist).

Swilsoo was supported and financed throughout (1993-2008) by the Swiss National Science Foundation, by means of six successive allocations of funds; it also received financial contributions from the cantonal governments of Geneva and Valais. We owe these institutions a debt of gratitude for their aid and their faith in our project.

REFERENCES

Bury, M., & Holme, A. (1991). *Life after ninety*. London & New York: Routledge.

Dupâquier, J., & Dupâquier, M. (1985). *Histoire de la démographie. La statistique de la population des origines à 1914*. Paris: Librairie académique Perrin.

Erikson, E. H. (1982). *The life cycle completed: A review*. New York: Norton.

Hofer, S. M., & Piccinin, A. M. (2007). Longitudinal studies. In J. E. Birren (Ed.), *Encyclopedia of gerontology: Age, aging, and the aged* (2nd ed.). Oxford: Elsevier Ltd.

Johnson, C. L., & Barer, B. M. (1997). *Life beyond 85 years. The aura of survivorship*. New York: Springer.

McClearn, G. E., Ahern, F., Berg, S., Johansson, B., Pedersen, N. L., Petrill, S. A., et al. (1997). Still heritable after all those years: Substantial genetic influence on cognitive ability in twins 80+ years old. *Science, 276*, 1560-1563.

Neugarten, B. L. (1974). Age groups in American society and the rise of the young old. *Annals of the American Academy of Political and Social Sciences, 415*, 187-198.

O'Connor, D. W., Pollitt, P. A., Hyde, J. B., Fellows, J. L., Miller, N. D., Brook, C. P. B., et al. (1989). The prevalence of dementia as measured by the Cambridge Mental Disorders of the Elderly Examination. *Acta Psychiatrica Scandinavica, 79*, 190-198.

Office Fédéral de la Statistique. (1996). *Tables de mortalité pour la Suisse*. Berne.

Romoren, T. I. (2003). *Last years of long lives, the Larvik study*. London: Routledge.

Romoren, T. I., & Blekeseaune, M. (2003). Trajectories of disability among the oldest old. *Journal of Aging and Health, 15*(3), 548-566.

Small, B. J., Basun, H., & Bäckman, L. (1998). Three-year changes in cognitive performance as a function of apolipoprotein E genotype: Evidence from very old adults without dementia. *Psychology and Aging, 13*, 80-87.

Snowdon, D. A., Kemper, S. J., & Mortimer, J. A. (1999). Linguistic ability in early life and cognitive function and Alzheimer's disease in late life: Findings from the Nun study. *Journal of the American Medical Association, 275*, 528-532.

Suzman, R. M., & Riley, M. (1985). The oldest old. *Milbank Memorial Fund Quarterly, 63*(2), 177-186.

Suzman, R. M., Willis, D. P., & Manton, K. G. (Eds.). (1992). *The oldest old*: Oxford University Press.

Svensson, T., Dehlin, O., Hagberg, B., & Samuelsson, G. (1993). The Lund 80+ study: Some general findings. In J. Schroots (Ed.), *Aging, health, and competence* (pp. 345-354). Amsterdam: Elsevier Science Publishers.

In: The Closing Chapters of Long Lives
Editors: E. Guilley, Ch. J. Lalive d'Epinay ISBN: 978-1-60456-971-1

Chapter 1

The Swiss Interdisciplinary Longitudinal Study on the Oldest-Old: Design and Population

Christian J. Lalive d'Epinay*[*], *Edith Guilley*, *Luc A. Guillet and Dario Spini

Abstract

The Swiss Interdisciplinary Longitudinal Study on the Oldest Old (Swilsoo) was designed to investigate life and health trajectories during advanced old age and their repercussions on elders' daily life. This chapter, divided in two sections, first introduces the reader to Swilsoo's design, samples and fieldwork. Two cohorts were assessed on an approximately yearly basis, the first for nine waves of interviews from 1994 to 2004, with 340 participants initially, and the second for five waves from 1999 to 2004, with 377 participants initially. The starting sample of each cohort was stratified by gender, age and geographical area (urban versus semi-rural) and was composed of community dwelling participants aged between 80 and 84 years; those who moved later to a nursing home remained in the study. Several aspects were assessed during the interviews (health, bereavement, social relationships and activities, well-being, cognitive ability, etc.). This chapter describes more specifically five main features of Swilsoo: 1) its 10-year longitudinal design; 2) its focus on the very old; 3) its dual focus on two birth cohorts; 4) the stratified and random selection of its participants; 5) its multidisciplinary and standardized closed-end questionnaire. A total of 2,890 questionnaires were gathered during the 10 years of the field work. The second section of the chapter gives an overview of the elders' life course through two world wars, the Great Depression, and later the Golden Decades (1946-1975); it then describes the survey population in terms of socioeconomic and cultural resources, family network and health, highlighting the main gender, geographical area and cohort differences.

---

[*] Correspondence concerning this chapter should be addressed to Christian J. Lalive d'Epinay, Center for Interdisciplinary Gerontology, Rte de Drize 7, Site Battelle, CH – 1227 Carouge, Christian.Lalive@socio.unige.ch

Sample, Design, and Field Work

Aims of the Study and Main Research Options Chosen

The design of an empirical study, which reflects the aims pursued, must be such as to make those aims attainable in optimum fashion. It must also take account of practical considerations including the funding available, the university institute's capacity to see a long-term project through to a successful conclusion, and the features specific to the target population.

In this chapter, we provide some indications on those various aspects. First of all, however, let us go straight to the heart of the matter and define the three main scientific objectives, which were:

(1) To track the principal health trajectories of advanced old age;
(2) To identify their repercussions on the way older people order their lives: their social relationships, their activities and forms of participation, and their well-being;
(3) To analyze the environmental, social and psychological factors that have a bearing on the health trajectories and on the elders' regulation of events and disruptions.

With those aims in view, the main strategic choices made were as follows:

(1) Since the study of trajectories calls for a *longitudinal strategy*, we opted for this solution, i.e. observation of a given population over a fairly long period of time in order to register the principal changes;
(2) Wishing to record health trajectories and life situations in all their diversity, we applied *stratified, random sampling* to the persons under study;
(3) As our focus was on people reaching or living through very old age, we decided to form two samples of persons aged 80 to 84 recruited from *two successive cohorts*, the samples being composed of persons belonging to a single five-year age class. The first, consisting of persons born between 1910 and 1914, was followed over a period of 10 years starting in 1994. Observations of the second, comprising persons born between 1915 and 1919, commenced in 1999 and ended five years later, in 2004.
(4) Retracing the trajectories followed by individuals in the various spheres of life demands comparable information gathered from respondents at each wave of interviews. We therefore favored systematic use of a *standardized questionnaire* containing mostly closed-end questions.

Let us now take a closer look at the options chosen.

A Ten-year Longitudinal Design

A sustained period of observation and data collection is needed in order to analyze life and health trajectories, hence our choice of a longitudinal research design. Unlike cross-sectional studies, longitudinal studies shed light on the path followed by each individual taking part in the survey. They have the drawback of being costly, however, because the interviews have to be repeated periodically, and time-consuming, because analysis cannot start until a certain threshold amount of data have been gathered. Funding sources are reluctant to guarantee financing over the long term.

Duration of Fieldwork

One decision we had to take thus related to the duration of the survey. A literature search revealed that a duration of at least five years was the minimum required to trace fragments of life trajectories, with their transitions and changes of direction in very old age.

We drew up a 10-year timetable but, to allow for practical contingencies, we split it into two five-year periods. The first period (1994-1999) was to cover longitudinal data collection on the first cohort (formed between 1910 and 1914) and sufficient data analysis to determine whether the results were promising enough to persuade the Swiss National Science Foundation (SNF) to finance the second phase. Our plan in that phase (1999-2004) was to prolong observations of the first cohort for another five years and to launch work on the second cohort (formed between 1915 and 1919). The intermediate results convinced the SNF and, thanks to its support, the full program could be carried through to completion.

Periodicity of Interview Waves

Closely linked with the question of fieldwork duration was that of the periodicity of interview waves. For practical and methodological reasons, a fairly brief interval seemed preferable, ideally one year or 18 months. A year may seem somewhat short. However, in the eyes of an octogenarian looking towards the future it is a lengthy span and a time in which many things can happen. For our survey, we felt that a relatively brief interval would greatly reduce the dropout risk. Regular contacts with the investigators create and strengthen the link between them and the respondents. If we add to that a clear explanation of the project and its aims at the outset and a short letter of thanks after each visit, if the investigators are motivated and prepared to spend an extra moment with the person when so invited, a closer relationship can be established with the elders, who then see themselves less as the objects of a survey and more as associates testifying to the human condition in advanced old age.

Methodologically speaking, the shorter interval enabled the team to record accurately the events and changes that had occurred since the previous visit. In this way, trajectories could be reconstituted and at a later stage antecedents and consequents distinguished in causal-type analyses. Table 1 summarizes the study's time line.

Table 1. Time line of the study

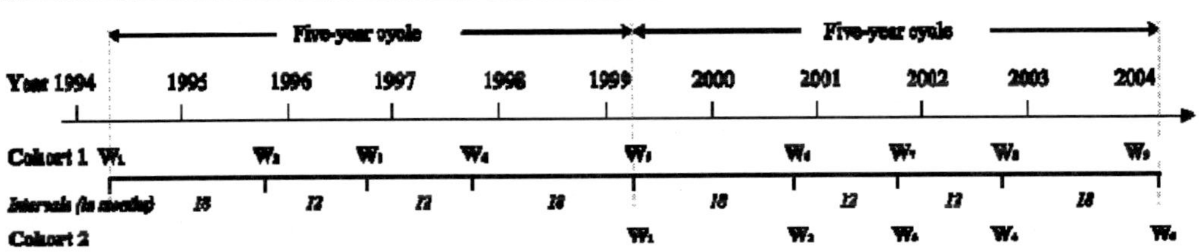

Random Sampling, Stratified by Gender, Geographical Area and Cohort

Stratification

The prime objective being to describe the elders' wide range of trajectories and life situations, we deemed it necessary to stratify the sample by three criteria: gender, geographical area and cohort.

Because of the difference in life expectancy, the population becomes more feminized as old age advances. In Switzerland, women make up 63% of the population in the 80-84 year age bracket, and 75% in the 90-94 year bracket (Swiss Federal Statistical Office, 2000). Stratification by gender is an essential precondition for a differential analysis of men's and women's trajectories.

By applying stratification by cohort[1] and choosing two contiguous cohorts, we were able to gauge the extent to which the results obtained were constant over time or conversely were influenced by cohort effects, in which case we sought to identify them.

The purpose of stratifying by two geographical areas was to obtain a clearer idea of the spatial diversity within the country. In particular, it brought to light the impact of the regional environment on the trajectories of old age. We opted for an urban/rural stratification by selecting two geographical areas, one that was typically urban at the time the cohort members were still in their childhood and the other rural and at first mainly agricultural but that later became gradually semi-rural, with a tertiary sector expanding thanks to tourism (Bassand, 1970). The former is the Canton of Geneva and the latter the central part of the Canton of Valais. The geographical contrast (one being situated on the plain and the other in the Alpine massif) echoes the contrast in their socioeconomic and cultural profiles. The Canton of Geneva forms part of one of the two main metropolitan regions in Switzerland, having a high population density (of 1,590 inhabitants per square kilometer in 1990), a large number of foreign residents, an essentially tertiary economy and a sizable public sector. The Valais, being a mountainous area, has a population density of only 84/sq km. Its heritage is one of farming, mountain life and Catholicism. Since the end of the 19th century and throughout the 20th, it has been the scene of various large-scale public works projects: railways and Alpine tunnels, then high-altitude dams. As from 1960, the boom in tourism saw villages mutating into winter sports resorts while economic activity veered sharply toward the service sector. Geneva, once strongly Calvinist, has become largely secular in culture, whereas Catholicism still prevails in the Alpine canton[2].

Random Selection

Only random selection of participants can guarantee the heterogeneous nature of the sample, i.e. representation of the widest possible range of social, cultural and health

---

[1] Age class and cohort are two approaches to the same operation of dividing up a population (e.g. the 80-84 year age class in 1994 is the 1910-1914 birth cohort). But the answers they provide are different. Age class, which circumscribes individuals by referring to their chronological age, is associated with enquiries into ageing and people's position in the life course (age roles etc.) ; the cohort, defined by a birth year marker, i.e. the point at which individuals join the march of history, is for its part associated with enquiries into the historical fate of all its members as a whole, and into the impact of the socio-historical environment and of biographies on individuals' present life situations. The period effect (i.e. effect of the calendar year) is not considered in this chapter.

[2] The terms metropolitan and urban are used synonymously in this book in referring to the Canton of Geneva, as are the terms semi-rural, Alpine and even rural as applied to the Canton of Valais.

conditions. Any other sampling method (calling for volunteers, choice of association members, the snowball sampling method, etc.) invariably culminates in the over-representation of some sectors of the population and under-representation of others.

Size of the Population Studied

The size of the samples used in longitudinal studies on the very old varied from 211[3] to 7447[4] persons (Hofer & Piccinin, 2007). In Swilsoo, the 1994 sample consisted of 340 persons (1st cohort) and that of 1999 (2nd cohort) 377, bringing the total number of elders to 717, with whom 2,890 interviews were conducted (see below). Some details are given in table 2.

Table 2. Sample at baseline (N, mean age, % of women and city-dwellers), by cohort

	N	Mean age (SD)	Women (%)	Urban (%)
Cohort 1	340	81.8 (1.4)	49.4	50.9
Cohort 2	377	81.9 (1.5)	50.1	49.1
Total	717	81.9 (1.4)	49.8	49.9

Choice of Starting Age: 80-84 Years

Choosing a starting age for the participants in the study was a delicate decision. What age would be best suited to studying an elder's progression and transitions in very old age? The first decision was to opt for members of a given five-year age class. The question then was: which age class should that be? According to demographers and epidemiologists, the transition from young old to oldest old takes place between the ages of 75 and 85 (the age bracket of the old old). However, these are probabilistic boundaries based on chronological age. For our purposes, it was necessary to define an age group in which relatively few persons suffer from serious functional incapacities but whose state of health is likely to change rapidly in the coming years. In order to do this, we looked again at the findings of a cross-sectional study that we had carried out in 1994 on the elderly population (aged 60 and over) in the same two geographical areas (Lalive d'Epinay, Bickel, Maystre, & Vollenwyder, 2000). Table 3 shows the distribution of this population by age class and by three levels of health status: ADL-dependent, ADL-independent frail and robust (definitions of which are given in chapter 2 of this book).

Up to the age of 75-79, most elders are robust and few ADL-dependent. In the following age group (80-84 years), the frail come into the majority, with ADL-dependent elders at around 20%. As we pass from this group to the next (85-89 years), a second inversion takes place, with the proportion of ADL-dependent persons rising steeply to overtake that of robust persons, which falls. Later, in the 90-94 year age group, there are slightly more ADL-dependent than ADL-independent frail, while the robust become the less prevalent category (although they still account for a heartening 15%!).

---

[3] Lund 80+ Study (Svensson, Dehlin, Hagberg, & Samuelsson, 1993)

[4] Asset and Health Dynamics Among the Oldest Old (AHEAD) (Myers, Juster, & Suzman, 1997)

We therefore decided in favor of the 80-84 year group as the starting age class and to limit the scope to community-dwelling elders. The reason for excluding nursing-home residents was that, in Switzerland, such persons are for the most part seriously disabled (Cavalli, 2002), whereas our aim was to focus on the conditions of entry into a situation of dependence. Moreover, because of their state of health, some are not able to answer interview questions, whereas we wanted to conduct at least the first interview directly with the person concerned, so as to establish a complete and homogeneous information base.

A Multidisciplinary and Standardized Closed-end Questionnaire

Information was gathered by means of a *standardized* questionnaire, consisting essentially of multiple choice questions (closed-end questionnaire). The questionnaire was submitted by the investigator at an interview held in a place of the elder's choice; in most cases, this meant the person's home. We ruled out telephone interviews partly because of the hearing difficulties of many persons of that age, and partly because we wanted to establish a long-term cooperative relationship with the elders and thus make personal contacts more congenial. The team of investigators was recruited and trained by our Center.

Certain specific characteristics of the very old led us to develop four versions of the basic questionnaire. For example, the person's state of health might have prevented him or her from taking part in an interview and answering questions. In such a case, abandoning the interview would have amounted to rejecting those in poorest health, thus skewing a study that was intended to trace health trajectories! To overcome this difficulty, we adopted the proxy method (Kapp, 1995). This allowed us to keep the elder among the participants and to limit, if not totally avoid, information loss, recognizing that facts can be reported by the proxy but the proxy's attitudes, opinions and appreciation of these facts do not necessarily coincide exactly with those of the older person in question.

Apart from the ability to take part in an interview, the elder's place of residence, whether at home or in an institution, has an impact on a whole set of questions concerning his or her physical and human environment. The questionnaire was therefore modified according to place of residence (community-dwelling or institutionalized) with two variants in each case, one for interviews with the elder and the other for interviews with the proxy.

Table 3. Distribution (%) of the elderly population by health status and age class

Age class	60-64	65-69	70-74	75-79	80-84	85-89	90-94
Robust	76.6	72.9	66.0	50.8	33.8	21.3	13.0
ADL-independent frail	22.5	25.6	29.9	41.0	45.6	44.7	37.0
ADL-dependent	0.9	1.5	4.1	8.2	20.6	34.0	50.0

Source: CIG, Cross-sectional data, 1994.

The interviewing strategy, and thus the overall organization of the questionnaire, was not the same at the first interview as at later interviews. The first interview provided the occasion to get to know the person and compile some basic information, including a series of biographical details. From the second interview onwards, the task was to update the person's file by scrupulously recording continuities and changes. The opening exchanges of the interview were therefore designed to establish a link with the previous one, the first question being:

"Since our last meeting (recalling the date and, if necessary, place), have there been any major changes in your life?"

This question situated the time period of relevance to the interview. As the questioning proceeded, information was gathered in the various fields of interest, either indirectly by asking the same questions as in the previous interview (e.g. on functional health), or directly, for example by asking the person if there had been any births (or deaths) in the family during the stated period. The topics covered in the interview related to facts (age, spatial mobility record since childhood, composition of family network, frequency of exchanges, illnesses and disabilities, daily activities, etc.), appraisals (of health, well being, past life), and attitudes or opinions (beliefs, views on society). The content of the questionnaire is shown in the annex to this chapter.

The questionnaire contained more than 600 questions in all and the interview lasted two hours on average. The proxy questionnaire contained just short of 200 questions and the interview seldom lasted more than three quarters of an hour.

In order to monitor attrition and its causes, we periodically checked the records of the civil registry to see if any deaths or changes of domicile had occurred and to note their date and place. We were thus able to maintain a complete record of mortality in the two samples, noting not only deaths of participants but also deaths of persons who had dropped out at one time or another. This kind of record compiled throughout the study period opens a number of avenues for scientific research, e.g. in the analysis of mortality predictors (Guilley, Pin, Spini, Lalive d'Epinay, Herrmann, & Michel, 2005).

Participation of Elders and Limitations of the Information Gathered

In this study, we sought the cooperation of octogenarians as eye-witnesses to life in advanced old age, an age that few attained in the past but that is becoming more accessible day by day, an age that has still to be mapped and whose real nature is little known. "Who better than you can tell what life is really like in advanced old age?" ran the letter urging them to accept our invitation, participation always being voluntary.

Information gathering was thus based on the elders' testimony regarding their own life including, as mentioned above, facts, appraisals and attitudes or opinions. This approach is unfortunately somewhat incompatible with the application of psychological tests, not to mention actual clinical examinations. Our preliminary enquiries had shown that, while the octogenarians were happy with the idea of contributing to a research project as witnesses, because this made them feel valuable and useful, they were reluctant to undergo tests for fear of failing or of being treated like a guinea-pig. Including batteries of tests in the questionnaire would not only have made it even longer but would also have triggered a higher refusal rate. The information gain would have been offset by plummeting sample numbers.

In preparing the Swilsoo project, we had initially thought of a two-pronged approach, one being the at-home interview based on the standard questionnaire and the other being a clinical-type interview with consenting elders. The latter interview would in principle have taken place in a teaching hospital and would have included cognitive as well as medical tests carried out by a health professional. This was the strategy adopted in the *Berlin Aging Study* launched in 1990 at the Max Planck Institute in Berlin under the direction of Paul Baltes and Karl-Ulrich Mayer. But a glance at the attrition rate tells all. Only 27% of persons who had answered the initial questionnaire were willing to go on to the next stage, even though a financial incentive was offered (Baltes & Mayer, 1999). As far as our project was concerned, we decided to drop the matter of tests, in view of the budget that would be required and the chances of securing it.

To sum up, the information presented in this book was provided by the elders themselves or, when this was not possible for reasons of disability, by proxies. That is the strength, as well as the limitation, of our study.

Survey Procedure and Final Results

Procedure

Table 4 shows how the fieldwork proceeded wave after wave. At the outset, the total population of the two cohorts of elders was 717. At the end of the five-year cycle, i.e. at wave 5, there remained 345 participants representing almost half (48.1%) of the original population. Two main causes lay behind the attrition rate of 51.9%. One was a natural cause, namely, death. Over the five-year period, 176 (91 in C1 and 85 in C2) elders, nearly a quarter (24.6%) of the initial number, died. The other was withdrawal from the project (sometimes under pressure from the family). A third, more technical, cause was a change of address when a person moved abroad or to a distant corner of Switzerland. Such cases were however very rare. In all, dropouts (with disappearances) represented 27.3% (77 in C1 and 119 in C2 on 717) of the starting sample. During the second five-year period (which concerned only the earlier cohort), deaths became more frequent, halving the number of those who had survived to the fifth wave (88 on 172). Dropouts were however few in number (25 on 172; 14.5%).

In table 4, it can be seen that, in both cohorts, the dropout rate was particularly high at the time of the second wave of interviews (1st cohort 13.2%, 2nd cohort 18.6%) and then dropped. This can be considered normal. Apparently, it is at the second round of conversations that the elder realizes the scope of his or her commitment and decides either to continue or to retract (Hansen, Tobler, & Graham, 1990).

The Dropouts

The dropout phenomenon – which cannot be avoided as long as participation is voluntary – raises a problem of methodology: do dropouts gradually inject bias into the sample and thus undermine its heterogeneity? Is the sociodemographic profile of the population modified, for instance, by large-scale defections of certain groups? Or could the health profile be altered, bearing in mind that declining health seems a logical reason for retracting?

Our analysis of the impact of dropouts on sample structure yielded the following results. As far as the sociodemographic profile is concerned, out of all the variables we had selected (gender, geographical area, social status, income, education, religion), only 'geographical area' showed a difference in dropouts, which were twice as numerous in the metropolitan

Table 4. Participants, deceased participants and dropouts, N (%), by cohort (C1, C2) and wave

		W1	W2	W3	W4	W5	*W1-W5*	W6	W7	W8	W9	*W6-W9*
C1	Year	1994	1995	1996	1997	1999	-	2000	2001	2002	2004	-
	Participants	340 (100.0)	267 (78.6)	237 (88.8)	209 (88.2)	172 (82.3)	*1225*	128 (74.4)	100 (78.1)	80 (80.0)	59 (73.8)	*367*
	Deceased	-	28 (8.2)	19 (7.1)	20 (8.4)	24 (11.5)	*91*	36 (20.9)	19 (14.8)	15 (15.0)	18 (22.5)	*88*
	Dropouts	-	45 (13.2)	11 (4.1)	8 (3.4)	13 (6.2)	*77*	8 (4.7)	9 (7.1)	5 (5.0)	3 (3.7)	*25*
	Total	340 (100.0)	340 (100.0)	267 (100.0)	237 (100.0)	209 (100.0)	-	172 (100.0)	128 (100.0)	100 (100.0)	80 (100.0)	-
C2	Year	1999	2000	2001	2002	2004	-					
	Participants	377 (100.0)	289 (76.7)	247 (85.5)	212 (85.8)	173 (81.6)	*1298*					
	Deceased	-	18 (4.7)	17 (5.9)	18 (7.3)	32 (15.1)	*85*					
	Dropouts	-	70 (18.6)	25 (8.6)	17 (6.9)	7 (3.3)	*119*					
	Total	377 (100.0)	377 (100.0)	289 (100.0)	247 (100.0)	212 (100.0)	-					
C1 + C2	Participants	717	556	484	421	345	-	172	128	100	80	-

canton. This result is not surprising because it is well known that withdrawal rates are higher in urban areas (Ribisl, Walton, Mowbray, Luke, Davidson II, & Bootsmiller, 1996). But since the dropout rate is not affected by the other variables, defections do not change the structure of the metropolitan sample and do not distort the findings. With regard to the health profile, contrary to what might be expected, dropouts were not more numerous among elders in poor health. In fact, defections by ADL-dependent persons were proportionally rarer than among others, the explanation being that the proxy arrangement worked extremely well, especially in nursing homes.

Fieldwork Results

With the first cohort, a total of 1,592 interviews were held, 1,225 at the first five waves and 367 at the last four. With the second, 1,298 interviews were held during the five years of the survey. The grand total was therefore 2,890 interviews (see table 4). The mean number of questionnaires filled out by cohort 1 participants was 4.7 (nine waves of interviews), and by cohort 2 participants 3.4 (five waves of interviews).

The proportion of questionnaires completed in nursing homes grew as time went by, amounting to 5.5% after five years (for both cohorts) and 11% after ten years for the first cohort. The percentage of questionnaires completed with the help of a proxy (in nursing homes or at private home) also rose: 8.9% at the first visit, 11.5% at the fifth, and 17.3% at the last. The vast majority of the 2,496 questionnaires (86.4%) were nevertheless filled out with the elders themselves.

Those figures should not mask the importance of the proxy method: without it, a total of 394 interviews could not have been conducted and we would have lost trace sooner of 194 elders.

But who were these proxies? When the elder was still living at home, the proxy in 35% of the cases was the spouse, in another 35% one of his or her offspring (usually a girl), and in 20% another member of the family. When the elder lived in a nursing home, the proxy in 58% of the cases was a member of the staff and in 42% a family member.

THE ELDERS: LIFE COURSE AND CURRENT SITUATION

A Generation's Progression through the 20th Century

The octogenarians of our study lived through almost the whole of the 20th century, a time of dramatic events and far-reaching socioeconomic and cultural changes. The Great War, the 1930's depression, World War II, then the Golden Decades of 1945-1975 and the growth of the welfare state, with the Cold War division of Europe (and the world) into two blocks – these were the salient events of their lives, now coming to an end amid the uncertainties of globalization.

They were born just before or during the Great War, following which the Spanish flu epidemic ravaged populations, especially the cohorts of our study. Switzerland was then far from being the rich country it was to become towards the middle of the century; as the year 1920 approached, the country still counted more than 600,000 destitutes among its 4 million inhabitants (Jost, 1983; Vuilleumier, 1973). Having spent their early years against a background of war, our cohort members were confronted in their adolescence by the Great Depression (1929-1932) when the older ones amongst them had to struggle to find a job. Poverty gave rise to rural-urban migration as well as emigration, to North and South America. While 80% of elders from the Alpine region had been born and grew up there, more than half of those from the metropolitan canton came to live there after their adolescence; some were of German or Italian mother tongue. The Second World War arrived when they were in their prime and the men were all called up for long periods of military service. This was an experience that the elders liked to recall: the long stints on guard at the frontier, waiting for a German invasion that fortunately never came. It was an epic time for those men, a time of hard work for the mothers and wives who stood in for the men at home and in the factories, an anxious time too, always listening for news on the radio.

Peace finally returned and was followed, to people's astonishment, by what later became known as the Golden Decades. This was a period of sustained, almost linear economic expansion, which brought with it full employment, a huge improvement in living standards and a plethora of new inventions and technologies, and which in time gave rise to a revolution in morals as well as in everyday life (Fourastié, 1979; Galbraith, 1958). In 1945, our cohort members were 26 to 35 years of age so in the course of their adult life they were able to take part in the grand endeavor to change the world and its living conditions. Then came talk of a post-industrial society (Bell, 1973; Touraine, 1969). The labor market was in effervescence; in the rural region, many farmers took jobs building high-altitude hydroelectric dams while others went to work in the factories springing up in the central valley, all of this in parallel to work on their own land. Amid the magnificent scenery of the Alps, the development of tourism, both winter and summer, kept pace with the overall growth of wealth. In the metropolitan region, the banking and service sector expanded rapidly, as did the public sector.

The steady rise in incomes endowed these cohorts with ever greater purchasing power, enabling them to take their place in the consumer society that was growing around them (Baudrillard, 1970). The sixties saw a steep rise in automobile ownership which, among its effects, brought an end to the isolation of villages. They also saw the arrival of domestic appliances and new materials such as plastics derived from petroleum, which eased household chores and made storage of foodstuffs easier (thanks to refrigerators and freezers). The seventies were the decade of television, a new medium for information and above all entertainment; they were also the decade of shortened working hours and new-found leisure and holiday opportunities, including foreign travel.

A feature of these decades of expansion was the development of social security (Fragnière & Girod, 2002; Maurer, 1982). In 1947, the Swiss people had voted overwhelmingly in favor of an old age insurance (OAI) law providing for a pension payable at the age of 65 for men and 62 – now 64 – for women. The pension was to be financed by a payroll levy shared between employer and employee. The guiding principle was one of mutual support (a) between generations, with those in work financing the pensions of the elderly, and (b) between income groups, the highest pension being only twice the lowest one whereas each actively employed person contributed a set percentage of his or her income. Initially, in the 1950's, the pension was modest but it was nevertheless a boon to the first generation of recipients, who had never expected it! As the years went by and economic growth continued, the pension level rose gradually, the goal being to provide people with the minimum amount needed to live. During the sixties, the so-called *Three Pillars* doctrine was formulated. The first pillar is the OAI legislation, which concerns all the resident population.

The second consists of a system of fully funded pension funds run by companies or sectors of economic activity. Together, the first and second pillars are intended to provide retirees with a decent standard of living. The third and last pillar is composed of private, voluntary savings. To this set of provisions was gradually added a system of additional entitlements for older people in straitened circumstances. However, it was not until 1982 that a federal law made contribution to corporate pension schemes compulsory for all categories of wage-earners, with the exception of the self-employed. In our cohort population, only 38% of the members received a pension, often an inadequate one, from a company scheme. The differences between geographical areas in this regard were considerable, with the rural region coming off worse (at 26%, compared with 50% for the urban region, partly reflecting the fact that farmers are self-employed and therefore not covered by the law on corporate pension schemes). Differences between genders were also great, to the advantage of men (42% compared with 32% for women). Just as the members of our cohorts were reaching retiring age, the oil crises of the early 1970's sounded the death knell of the Golden Decades. However, the nature of the Swiss job market was such that full employment was maintained until about 1990. Many people went on working for a few years beyond the age of 65, encouraged to do so by an employer short of manpower but also by the meagerness of their retirement pensions. But as corporate schemes gradually increased their coverage, retirement at the legal age became mandatory. In parallel to these developments, with lengthening life expectancies and ageing populations, the cantonal authorities introduced other measures. At first, retirement homes mushroomed then, as the 1980's drew near, the cantons of our two survey populations adopted policies aimed at encouraging community living, buttressed by greatly strengthened home care and aid services.

How did the demographic situation of these two cohorts look as the members turned 80? Death had been unsparing. Of the men, one in four was still alive, and of the women four in ten. Thus when Swilsoo was set in motion, the elders involved were already survivors! To give a point of comparison, demographers predict that in the cohort of 1970 (who are thus 60 years younger) 65% of men and 80% of women will be able to greet the year 2050 as they pass the 80-year milestone! (Menthonnex & Wanner, 1998).

Present Situation: Regional Similarities and Differences in Gender and Cohort

We have now described in broad lines our survey population's collective experience. Let us now dwell for a moment on some of the attributes shared by its members, some features of their life situation at the outset of the study, and the main differences that distinguished them by area of residence, gender and cohort.

The level of education of that generation reflected the schooling situation in the inter-war period, but the degree to which youngsters were encouraged to study varied greatly by canton and by gender. In the Alpine region, slightly less than half (47%) of the men and three quarters (77%) of the women completed only the compulsory curriculum; in the metropolitan region, the figures were 21% and 43%, respectively. The socio-occupational structures were also contrasting. The elders of the rural region were mostly manual workers: farmers, laborers and tradesmen. A mere 37% of them were white-collar workers, whereas the equivalent figure in the metropolitan region was 62%.

That generation was deeply imbued with religion. With very few exceptions (encountered in the metropolitan region only) all had a religious education and were baptized and married in church. The Alpine region is Catholic and in its cohorts almost all (90%) were regular churchgoers. In Geneva, the home of Calvin, there has been separation of church and State since the beginning of the 19th century. Because of immigration, Catholics were in the minority in our cohorts (38% versus 53% for Protestants). Church attendance was less widespread than in the rural region but nearly six out of ten city-dwellers none the less attended regularly. The strongly religious culture of that generation contrasted with the culture of later generations, which have been drifting away from the major Christian faiths since the 1960's (Lalive d'Epinay & Spini, 2004) (For the Swiss case, see Campiche & Broquet, 2004).

The Alpine canton's Catholicism finds an echo in the number of children per family: only 17% had no offspring, whereas in the metropolitan canton the proportion was 25%. Of those who did have descendants, the average number of children was 3.6 compared with 2.2. Even greater differences are to be found in the number of siblings. The upshot of these differences is that elders of the Alpine region had much more extensive family networks.

In 1994, when the study started, the marital status profile was roughly the same in the two regions, except that in the metropolitan canton 7% of the elders were divorced or separated whereas this situation was very rare in the Alpine canton (1.4%!), another mark of its religious values. The profiles of men and women were very different, however: seven men out of ten still had their spouse but only one woman in four! This induced a corresponding difference in situations of everyday life: 62% of women lived alone but only 23% of men. In the urban region, 25% of elders had no (or no longer had any) children, 35% had no grandchildren or great grandchildren, and 39% no siblings; in the other geographical area, the figures were 17%, 25% and 23%, respectively, and here the differences by gender were minimal. The family network was larger in the Alpine region, lessening the risk of isolation.

The elders' financial situation differed greatly from one geographical area to the other, the average monetary income being lower in the Alpine region. Most of them did however own land. Three quarters of them (72%) were homeowners, which was the case for only a quarter (24%) of the city-dwellers. Seven out of ten possessed orchards, vineyards, kitchen gardens or grazing land. In the urban canton, only three out of ten owned land, and in most cases it was not farmland but a yard. Being a homeowner saves money. It is also psychologically reassuring, especially when, as now, property speculation is rife. Land, for its part, is a source of produce that can be consumed at home or exchanged with others. These two types of resources (monetary and physical) engendered a disparity between geographical areas. In the metropolitan canton, more than half (56%) of the elders lived in comfort while a minority (13%) were poor; in the semi-rural region, midway situations were the rule, both poverty and riches being rare. In both geographical areas, however, it was very largely the women, especially widows, who were poor. The reasons for this are touched on above.

While the great majority of inhabitants in the semi-rural canton owned their own home, access to that home could become a problem with age ; in 60% of cases access was via stairs (versus 27% in the urban region). Moreover, 11% did not have all the modern conveniences at home (toilet, bathroom, central heating, hot water and refrigerator); in the other geographical area the figure was 4%. Also, unlike the urban canton with its highly developed public transport system, the rural region is mountainous and its towns and villages scattered, making journeys difficult for older people.

What of the health status of these octogenarians at baseline? We have data on their *physical pains* (cf. chapter 2), their *functional health* (5 basic ADL, 3 mobility items, 4 items concerning hearing and sight ; cf. chapters 2 and 3), and their *well-being (*cf. chapters 8, 9), as well as a five-degree measure of *self-rated health* (cf. chapters 8, 9).

About half (52%) of the octogenarians did not suffer from physical pains, and that was true for both geographical areas, for men and for women. As regards functional health, few (8%) were ADL-dependent but to these must be added persons declaring that they had difficulty in accomplishing basic activities unaided (12%). In addition, nearly four in ten had diminished mobility, a third or more had trouble following a conversation, and one in five had problems of eyesight.

Because of the decision we made in our initial sampling (to exclude institutionalized persons), octogenarians requiring assistance to perform the basic activities of daily living were few in number at the outset, but there were already many for whom going out had become a hazardous enterprise. For some, reading had become difficult; for a greater number of others, it was their hearing that had deteriorated. Poor hearing is often felt to be a cause of exclusion; people feel isolated in a group when they cannot keep up with the conversation. The signs of a shrinking living space (mobility), restricted activities (reading) and relational isolation (hearing) were all present, even if at that stage they did not apply to the majority (Lalive d'Epinay & Guilley, 2006).

Most of the octogenarians had a satisfactory level of well-being. Almost all stated that they had pleasure in doing things (96%), that they were self-confident (92%), and that they were hopeful about the future (78%). The negative affects most often quoted were anxiety (16%), loneliness (14%), sadness (11%) and boredom (10%). When asked about their health (*self-rated health*), over half of the elders considered it good (38%) or very good (18%), only one in ten considered it bad, and 34% considered it satisfactory. It should be pointed out that declaring one's health to be satisfactory comes down to saying that one has to make the best of it, and thus implies some misgivings.

Women and men differed little as regards health except psychologically, more women than men exhibiting depressive symptoms. The health profiles of the octogenarians were also fairly similar in the two geographical areas. The only difference was in functional health, where there were twice as many elders suffering from disabilities or functional difficulties in the Alpine region, a consequence of their past working and living conditions.

Conclusions

The octogenarians' profiles in the two geographical areas reflect the regions' socioeconomic and culturo-religious differences. As we have seen, these show up in the sources of income, in the quality of housing, and in the size of family networks. In the Alpine region, the higher proportion of manual workers, particularly of those engaged in small-scale mountain farming, accounted for the greater percentage of persons suffering from functional disabilities.

A comparison of men and women brings to light not mere differences but real inequalities, which weigh on women in very old age. The vast majority of them live alone, their situation is materially less comfortable than that of men, and it is essentially they who make up the pockets of poverty in advanced old age. However, at the outset of the study, their health status was no different to that of men, except for their greater tendency to report depressive symptoms (Our initial data were thus at odds with the prevailing theory that women, who have a longer life expectancy than men, are disadvantaged by poorer health. However, in our study, gaps between the genders appeared as the years went by (Guilley, Guillet, & Girardin, in press).

What then of the comparison between the two cohorts of octogenarians involved in the study? As they were separated by an interval of only five years, it would have been surprising to find any marked differences of the order of those pertaining to the geographical areas or genders. And yet, a series of minor but statistically significant changes can be discerned in the later cohort: better level of education, higher proportion of white-collar workers and upper middle class persons, materially better living conditions in terms of income as well as home comfort, fewer poor, and improved health (better self-rated health, fewer persons suffering from functional disabilities and depressive symptoms). Furthermore, even though the differences between geographical areas and between men and women are still pronounced, some narrowing can be seen.

These changes in the conditions of existence from one cohort to the other are the reflection at a personal level of the economic and social development – the "progress" – that took place in industrial societies during the 20th century. As demonstrated elsewhere (Lalive d'Epinay et al., 2000), this relatively linear progression proved durable, bringing benefits to successive cohorts up to 1950-1960. Nevertheless, it is by no means impossible that, under the effect of the economic and social changes brought about by globalization, a reversal of this trend may already be under way, an assertion that will have to wait for a study of later cohorts in old age to be confirmed.

ANNEX. THE QUESTIONNAIRE: SECTION HEADINGS AND DATA ITEMS

Heading	Items recorded
Status variables	Gender, year of birth, place of birth, marital status Education and post-school qualifications Socio-occupational status (before retirement)
Biographical details	Place of birth and of childhood Language of childhood Residential trajectory Matrimonial and family trajectory Health trajectory Occupational and retirement trajectory
Living circumstances	Nature of domicile: private / institution; Living in an apartment / house; Owner / tenant / in other's home Environment: city / town or village / isolated Number of rooms, conveniences Means of transport

Financial situation	Assets, income Non-monetary resources Insurance coverage and social benefits
Household	In own home : composition of household
Health	Illnesses / physical pains / functional status / sensory capacities Self-rated health (per se; by comparison) Well-being: depressive symptoms Illnesses and health-related incidents (since previous visit): periods of confinement to bed, falls, hospitalization Consumption of care: medical check-ups, dental care, medication Habits involving risk, preventive behavior : alcohol and tobacco consumption / physical activities and exercises *If cohabitant*: his / her functional status
Institutional network	Use made of institutional network : nature and frequency of services
Family network	Family size and composition Proximity of offspring, siblings Frequency of exchanges Support provided and received: frequency and nature
Friendship network	Existence of a close friend Frequency of exchanges Support provided and received: frequency and nature Neighborhood relations
Activities, social and cultural life	Activities : nature and periodicity Use made of the media : nature of media, frequency Participation in associations Religious activity
Psychosocial dimensions	Check on cognition Self-assessment of health Coping Beliefs and values Perception of important changes in life since last interview

REFERENCES

Baltes, P. B., & Mayer, K. U. (1999). *The Berlin Aging Study: Aging from 70 to 100*. New York, USA: Cambridge University Press.

Bassand, M. (1970). *Métropolisation et inégalités sociales*. Lausanne: Presses polytechniques et universitaires romandes.

Baudrillard, J. (1970). *La société de consommation*. Paris: Gallimard.

Bell, D. (1973). *The coming of post-industrial society*. London: Heinemann.

Campiche, R. J., & Broquet, R. (2004). *Les deux visages de la religion: fascination et désenchantement*. Genève: Editions Labor et Fides.

Cavalli, S. (2002). *Vieillards à domicile, vieillards en pension: une comparaison [Elderly at home, elderly in a nursing home: A comparison]*. Lausanne: Réalités Sociales

Fourastié, J. (1979). *Les Trente Glorieuses*. Paris: Fayard.

Fragnière, J. P., & Girod, R. (Eds.). (2002). *Dictionnaire Suisse de politique sociale (2e édition révisée)*. Lausanne: Réalités Sociales.

Galbraith, J. K. (1958). *The affluent society*. Boston, MA: Houghton.

Guilley, E., Guillet, L., & Girardin, M. (in press). Does the gender paradox persist in the last years of very long lives? In H. T. Benninghouse, & A. G. Rosset (Eds.), *Women and Aging: New Research*. Hauppauge, NY: Nova Science Publishers, Inc.

Guilley, E., Pin, S., Spini, D., Lalive d'Epinay, C., Herrmann, F. R., & Michel, J.-P. (2005). Association between social relationships and survival of Swiss octogenarians. A five-year prospective, population-based study. *Aging Clinical and Experimental Research, 17*(5), 419-425.

Hansen, W. B., Tobler, N. S., & Graham, J. W. (1990). Attrition in substance abuse prevention research: A Meta-Analysis of 85 Longitudinally Followed Cohorts. In R. A. Berk (Ed.), *Evaluation Review* (Vol. 14, pp. 677-685). Los Angeles: Sage Publications, Inc.

Hofer, S. M., & Piccinin, A. M. (2007). Longitudinal studies. In J. E. Birren (Ed.), *Encyclopedia of gerontology: Age, aging, and the aged* (2nd ed.). Oxford: Elsevier Ltd.

Jost, H.-U. (1983). Menace et repliement:1914-1945. In *Nouvelle histoire de la Suisse et des Suisses* (Vol. III, pp. 91-178). Lausanne: Payot.

Kapp, M. B. (1995). Proxy decision making. In G. L. Maddox (Ed.), *The Encyclopedia of Aging, Second Edition* (pp. 771-772). New York: Springer Publishing Company.

Lalive d'Epinay, C., Bickel, J.-F., Maystre, C., & Vollenwyder, N. (2000). *Vieillesses au fil du temps. 1979-1994: une révolution tranquille [Old age across the years. 1979-1994: A quiet revolution]*. Lausanne: Réalités sociales.

Lalive d'Epinay, C., & Guilley, E. (2006). Statuts de santé et mondes de vie quotidienne des vieillards [Health Statuses and Everyday Life-Worlds among oldest-old People]. *Swiss Journal of Sociology, 32*(3), 407-427.

Lalive d'Epinay, C., & Spini, D. (2004). Religion and health: A European perspective. In K. W. Schaie, N. M. Krause, & A. Booth (Eds.), *Religious influences on health and well-being in the elderly* (pp. 44-58). New York, NY: Springer Publishing Company, Inc.

Maurer, A. (1982). La Suisse. In P. A. Köhler, & H. F. Zacher (Eds.), *Un siècle de sécurité sociale. L'évolution en Allemagne, France, Grande-Bretagne, Autriche et Suisse* (pp. 525-612). Nantes: CRHES.

Menthonnex, J., & Wanner, P. (1998). *Tables de mortalité longitudinales pour la Suisse. Genération 1880-1980*. Bern: Swiss Federal Statistical Office.

Myers, D. G., Juster, F. T., & Suzman, R. M. (1997). Asset and health dynamics among the oldest old (AHEAD): Initial results from the longitudinal study. *Journal of Gerontology: Social Sciences, 52B*(Special issue), 1-8.

Ribisl, K. M., Walton, M. A., Mowbray, C. T., Luke, D. A., Davidson II, W. S., & Bootsmiller, B. J. (1996). Minimizing participant attrition in panel studies through the use of effective retention and tracking strategies: Review and recommendations. *Evaluation and Program Planning, 19*(1), 1-25.

Svensson, T., Dehlin, O., Hagberg, B., & Samuelsson, G. (1993). The Lund 80+ study: Some general findings. In J. Schroots (Ed.), *Aging, health, and competence* (pp. 345-354). Amsterdam: Elsevier Science Publishers.

Swiss Federal Statistical Office. (2000). The 2000 population census. 2008, from http://www.bfs.admin.ch/bfs/portal/fr/index.html

Touraine, A. (1969). *La société post-industrielle.* Paris: Denoël.

Vuilleumier, M. (1973). Quelques jalons pour une historiographie du mouvement ouvrier en Suisse. *Cahiers Vilfredo Pareto : revue européenne des sciences sociales, XI*(29), 5-35.

PART 1: ARCHITECTURE OF VERY OLD AGE: PATTERNS OF HEALTH TRAJECTORIES

In: The Closing Chapters of Long Lives
Editors: E. Guilley, Ch. J. Lalive d'Epinay

ISBN: 978-1-60456-971-1

Chapter 2

INDIVIDUAL HEALTH TRANSITIONS BETWEEN ROBUSTNESS, ADL-INDEPENDENT FRAILTY AND ADL-DEPENDENCE IN LATE LIFE

Edith Guilley*[*]*, Paolo Ghisletta, Franca Armi, André Berchtold and Christian J. Lalive d'Epinay

ABSTRACT

While frailty has often been assumed to be a transitional state between robustness and ADL-dependence, no research has supported this assumption with empirical data. This study documents individual health trajectories in order to assess whether frailty (a) can be considered as a necessary precursor to ADL-dependence, (b) is of short duration or long-lasting and, (c) is reversible or irreversible. The octogenarians participating in the Swiss Interdisciplinary Longitudinal Study on the Oldest Old were assessed a maximum of nine times over ten years. The transitions between robustness (non-frail persons without ADL incapacities), ADL-independent frailty (frail without ADL incapacities) and ADL-dependence (frail with one ADL incapacity or more) were analyzed using Markov chain methods. At baseline, 42.4%, 49.4% and 8.1% of the sample were classified respectively as robust, ADL-independent frail, and ADL-dependent. Among those who became ADL-dependent, 76.6% were ADL-independent frail at the previous wave. Stability was the predominant pattern for ADL-independent frail people: on the average 58.8% of them maintained the same health status at the following wave. Recovery from ADL-independent frailty was possible (17.9%) but was often of short duration: among ADL-independent frail persons who recovered to become robust, 51.9% became ADL-independent frail again one wave later. Frailty was the dominant health status in these very elderly individuals and can be considered as a relatively long transitional period between robustness and ADL-dependence. Recovery from ADL-independent frailty to robustness occurs but appears to be quite short-lived.

[*] Correspondence concerning this chapter should be addressed to Edith Guilley, Center for Interdisciplinary Gerontology, Rte de Drize 7, Site Battelle, CH – 1227 Carouge, edith.guilley@orange.fr

INTRODUCTION

In the recent literature, frailty is conceptualized as a multi-system reduction in reserve capacity (e.g. Fried, 1994). Frail elderly people, due to the decrease in their reserve capacity, exhibit vulnerability to medical, psychosocial and environmental stressors and are unable to regain equilibrium with the surrounding environment after a major disturbing event such as a fall, an acute illness or an emotional upheaval (cf. Hamerman, 1999; Rockwood, 1997; Spini, Ghisletta, Guilley, & Lalive d'Epinay, 2007). Consequently, frail elderly individuals are at higher risk of developing adverse health outcomes, including severe ADL or IADL disabilities and ADL-dependence (Bandeen-Roche et al., 2006; Fried et al., 2001; Guilley et al., 2008). This has led some researchers to consider frailty as a transitional stage between a state of robustness and a rather critical situation of functional dependence (e.g. Speechley & Tinetti, 1991).

The aim of this chapter is to document individual transitions between robustness, frailty and ADL-dependence. Although frailty has been shown to lead to adverse health outcomes, it has not yet been demonstrated whether or not frailty is a necessary precursor to ADL-dependence. In other terms, were all ADL-dependent individuals previously frail? Another unanswered question in the gerontological literature is whether the transition from frailty to ADL-dependence is a lasting situation or one of short duration. Does this transition occur in a smooth and gradual manner or is there an avalanche-like decline in different health dimensions? Lastly, previous research has investigated whether some factors contributing to frailty, such as functional capacity, are reversible (Binder et al., 2002). However to our knowledge, no study has yet tested whether frailty as a whole is reversible and no proof of its reversibility is currently available. These key questions concerning the duration of frailty, its potential reversibility, and its role as a forerunner to ADL-dependence can only be answered by means of empirical data based on repeated measures at the individual level rather than single assessments at the group level. Longitudinal research designs (preferably long-term) are thus required (cf. Spini et al., 2007).

Using a population of Swiss octogenarians assessed up to nine times over ten years, we propose here to examine whether frailty can be considered as a process leading from robustness to ADL-dependence. In particular, we examine whether frailty (a) is necessarily a precursor to ADL-dependence, (b) is of short duration or long-lasting in nature and (c) is reversible or not.

METHOD

Participants

All participants in the two cohorts of the Swiss Interdisciplinary Longitudinal Study on the Oldest Old (Swilsoo) were considered (N = 717; 2,890 total interviews across all waves of the study). Please see chapter 1 for a description of the sample.

Health Measures

Health status was classified as either ADL-dependent, ADL-independent frail, or robust. A participant was considered ADL-dependent if he/she was unable to perform alone at least one of five activities of daily living (washing, dressing and undressing, eating, rising from and going to bed, and moving from one room to another; cf. Katz, Ford, Moskowitz, Jackson, & Jaffee, 1963). Participants without ADL-incapacities but suffering from two or more deficiencies in five health domains (sensoriality, mobility, memory, energy and physical ailments; cf. appendix) were considered as ADL-independent frail. Finally, participants having no ADL incapacities and fewer than two deficiencies in the five health domains were considered as robust (for further details, see Guilley et al., 2008).

Analysis Strategies

We documented all possible transitions between robustness, ADL-independent frailty and ADL-dependence. Because probabilities of health status transitions were not specific to the period under observation, we studied the dependence between any successive observations with homogeneous Markov chain models (cf. Berchtold & Raftery, 2002). A first model, of first-order, was based on eight, two-consecutive-wave periods (i.e., periods between waves 1-2, 2-3, 3-4, etc. up to 8-9); and a second model of second-order on seven, three-consecutive-wave periods (i.e. 1-2-3, 2-3-4, 3-4-5, etc. up to 7-8-9). This methodology is particularly appealing because of its flexibility (e.g., no particular distributions are required). All associated probabilities of transitions with their confidence intervals were estimated using the MARCH 2.10 software (Berchtold, 2004). Because cohort analyses revealed no health effects, we merged the two cohorts into a single analysis.

RESULTS

At baseline, 42.4%, 49.4% and 8.1% of the sample were classified respectively as robust, ADL-independent frail, and ADL-dependent. Nine waves later (equivalent to ten years), the sample comprised 20.3% robust, 47.5% ADL-independent frail, and 32.2% ADL-dependent participants.

To analyze individual health trajectories at any two successive waves of our study, we applied Markov chain methods. Table 1 summarizes the results of a first-order Markov model by presenting the counts and percentages of all health status transitions over any two successive waves. The rows represent the three origin states, in the form of the three health statuses at any wave *Wn*. The columns represent the four destination states, at wave *Wn+1*, namely the three health statuses and death (which can only be conceived as a destination status). The total number of two-wave transitions is 2,407 (participants assessed only once cannot be included in this analysis).

Table 1. Health status transitions (n = 2,407) between any two successive waves

	Destination health status at wave *Wn+1*				
Origin health status at wave *Wn*, N (row %)	Robust	ADL-independent frail	ADL-dependent	Deceased	Precision coefficient[1]
Robust	558 (62.1)	257 (28.6)	43 (4.9)	41 (4.6)	3.8
ADL-independent frail	195 (17.9)	639 (58.8)	141 (13.0)	112 (10.3)	3.4
ADL-dependent	14 (3.3)	48 (11.4)	250 (59.4)	109 (25.9)	5.5

[1] Precision coefficient corresponds to one half-confidence interval around the four percentages in that row (e.g., for a percentage estimated at 62.1 a precision of 3.8 computed with a type I risk of alpha=5% gives a confidence interval ranging from 58.3 (62.1-3.8) to 65.9 (62.1+3.8)).

Overall, we observe that stability was the predominant pattern. Of the robust, the ADL-independent frail and the ADL-dependent, 62.1% (95% confidence interval = 58.3-65.9), 58.8% (95% CI = 55.4-62.2) and 59.4% (95% CI = 53.9-64.9), respectively, were in the same health category at the following wave. Of the ADL-independent frail 13.0% (95% CI = 9.6-16.4) became ADL-dependent at wave *Wn+1*, while 17.9% (95% CI = 14.5-21.3) recovered to become robust. An analysis of these resilient cases revealed that the reversibility was mainly due to recovery from problems of energy, physical pains or sensory functioning. Among those who became ADL-dependent at wave *Wn+1*, the majority had previously been ADL-independent frail (76.6% = 141 / (141+43)). This situation may hence constitute a transition category between robustness and ADL-dependence. Lastly, we observe that, among the ADL-independent frail, the transition to death was as likely as the transition to ADL-dependence.

Figure 1 presents a selection of results from the second-order Markov chains, specifically, the health statuses which followed the transition from frailty to robustness. Recovery to robustness did occur but was most often of short duration. Indeed, among ADL-independent frail persons who recovered to become robust, 51.9% (95% CI, 43.0-60.8) became ADL-independent frail again one wave later (cf. Figure 1).

Discussion

This study was motivated by three questions: (a) Is frailty a necessary precursor to ADL-dependence? (b) Is frailty of short duration or is it a lasting situation? (c) Is frailty reversible? Our analyses revealed that the majority of individuals becoming ADL-dependent had transited through ADL-independent frailty. In other words, frailty is a highly probable precursor to ADL-dependence. However, even if ADL-dependence is the likely consequence of the latest stage of growing frailty process (Bandeen-Roche et al., 2006; Fried, 1994; Guilley et al., 2008), it is not the sole outcome of frailty. Our results indicated that, among the ADL-independent frail, the transition to death was as likely as the transition to ADL-dependence. Thus for some of the frail elderly, mortality may avoid the experience of ADL-dependence. ADL-dependence is not necessarily the life stage that precedes death, as previously discussed by Lalive d'Epinay (2004).

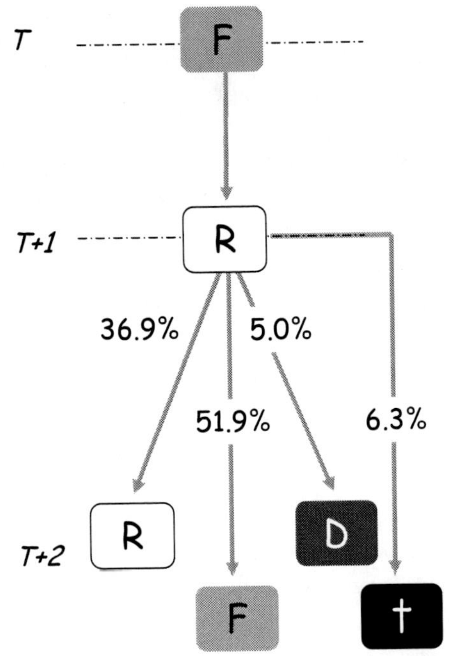

Notes: the precision coefficient around the four percentages is equal to 8.9%; R, F, D, and † correspond respectively to robust, ADL-independent frail, ADL-dependent, and deceased individuals.

Figure 1. Health statuses following a transition from ADL-independent frailty to robustness (n = 160).

Our findings demonstrate that the stage of frailty is not likely to be short-lived. In our sample, most individuals considered ADL-independent frail at any point in time still had the same health status 12 to 18 months later. This indicates that, for a majority of octogenarians, ADL-independent frailty can be a lasting situation and does not necessarily entail a rapid decline towards ADL-dependence or death.

Another important feature of the frailty process is its reversibility. The transition from ADL-independent frailty to robustness occurred in 18% of the octogenarians. However, additional analyses at three successive waves indicated that this recovery was followed by a health deterioration in 63.1% of the cases. This suggests, as postulated by Anderson, James, Miller, Worley, and Longino (1998) in their study on functional status transitions, that for some elderly persons positive transitions may indicate instability (or at best short-lasting respite) rather than full recovery. In sum, then, the transitional period of frailty intervening between robustness and ADL-dependence is likely to be lengthy and not necessarily unidirectional, although reversal is not the dominant pattern, and when it occurs it is of short duration. Therefore, future research should examine not only how to delay the onset of frailty but also how to lengthen the period of recovery from frailty by promoting active intervention strategies such as nutritional programs, physical exercise training, healthy lifestyles and supportive care.

Our findings, although instructive, are affected by a few limitations. In spite of the use of proxy reports, 16.0% of participants refused to continue with the study between baseline and wave 2. This percentage fell to 3.8-7.8% in subsequent waves. It is possible that the health transitions of these dropouts would have been different from those of the participants assessed longitudinally. Indeed, poorer physical health is usually one of the strongest predictors of dropout in gerontological research, not only in Swilsoo (Ghisletta & Spini, 2004). Secondly, while the model based on aggregated 3-wave health transitions did provide complementary information, it necessarily applied to fewer, albeit longer, segments of trajectories and hence was less precise in estimation compared to the model based on aggregated 2-wave health transitions. Similarly, Markov chain models with a higher order would reduce precision further due to the diminishing number of these types of transition chains. As interpretation of highly imprecise probabilities is problematic, the models of an order greater than 2 were not developed. Thirdly, the results were based partly on proxy reports, which may reflect what caregivers allow the participants to do rather than their actual capacities (Ferrucci, Guralnik, Studenski, Fried, Cutler, & Walston, 2004). However, proxy bias was probably minor because our findings were virtually identical when proxy reports were excluded from the analyses.

In our aging cohort of octogenarians, we found that ADL-independent frailty was the dominant health status and can be considered as a relatively long transitional period between robustness and ADL-dependence. Recovery from ADL-independent frailty to robustness occurs but appears to be quite short-lived. The timely diagnosis of frailty and/or the lengthening of periods of recovery from frailty remain a major individual and public health challenge.

Appendix. List of Domains and Items Used to Evaluate Frailty

Sensory		
Difficulty	1/ reading a newspaper	
	2/ hearing in a conversation with another person	
	3/ hearing in a conversation with several persons	
Mobility		
Difficulty	1/ going up and down stairs	
	2/ moving around outside	
	3/ walking 200 meters	
Physical pains		
Suffering a lot of pain in	1/ lower limbs	
	2/ upper limbs	
	3/ head, face	
	4/ back	
	5/ heart	
	6/ respiratory organs	
	7/ stomach, abdomen	
	8/ genital, urinary organs	
Memory		
	Frequent problems with memory	
Energy		
	Frequent tiredness	
	Frequent loss of appetite	

Note: Individuals having a problem with at least one item of the five domains were considered to have a deficiency in that particular domain.

References

Anderson, R. T., James, M. K., Miller, M. E., Worley, A. S., & Longino, C. F. (1998). The timing of change: Patterns in transitions in functional status among elderly persons. *Journal of Gerontology: Social Sciences, 53B*(1), S17-S27.

Bandeen-Roche, K., Xue, Q.-L., Ferrucci, L., Walston, J. D., Guralnik, J. M., Chaves, P., et al. (2006). Phenotype of frailty: Characterization in the women's health and aging studies. *Journal of Gerontology: Medical Sciences, 61A*(3), 262-266.

Berchtold, A. (2004). MARCH version 2.11: Retrieved from http://www.andreberchtold.com/march.html.

Berchtold, A., & Raftery, A. (2002). The mixture transition distribution model for high-order Markov chains and non-Gaussian time series. *Statistical Science, 17*(3), 328-356.

Binder, E. F., Schechtman, K. B., Ehsani, A. A., Steger-May, K., Brown, M., Sinacore, D. R., et al. (2002). Effects of exercise training on frailty in community-dwelling older adults: Results of a randomized, controlled trial. *Journal of the American Geriatrics Society, 50*(12), 1921-1928.

Ferrucci, L., Guralnik, J. M., Studenski, S., Fried, L. P., Cutler, G. B., & Walston, J. D. (2004). Designing randomized, controlled trials aimed at preventing or delaying functional decline and disability in frail, older persons: A consensus report. *Journal of the American Geriatrics Society, 52*, 625-634.

Fried, L. P. (1994). Frailty. In W. R. Hazzard, E. L. Bierman, J. P. Blass, W. H. J. Ettinger, & J. B. Halter (Eds.), *Principles of geriatric medicine and gerontology, 4th ed* (pp. 1149-1156). McGraw Hill, New York.

Fried, L. P., Tangen, C. M., Walston, J. D., Newman, A. B., Hirsch, C., Gottdiener, J., et al. (2001). Frailty in older adults: Evidence for a phenotype. *Journal of Gerontology: Medical Sciences, 56A*(3), M146-M156.

Ghisletta, P., & Spini, D. (2004). An introduction to generalized estimating equations and an application to assess selectivity effects in a longitudinal study on very old individuals. *Journal of Educational and Behavioral Statistics, 29*(4), 423-439.

Guilley, E., Ghisletta, P., Armi, F., Berchtold, A., Lalive d'Epinay, C., Michel, J.-P., et al. (2008). Dynamics of frailty and ADL-dependence in a five-year longitudinal study of octogenarians. *Research on Aging, 30*(3), 299-317.

Hamerman, D. (1999). Toward an understanding of frailty. *Annals of Internal Medicine, 130*(11), 945-950.

Katz, S., Ford, A. B., Moskowitz, R. W., Jackson, B. A., & Jaffee, M. W. (1963). Studies of illness in the aged. The index of ADL: A standardized measure of biological and psychosocial function. *Journal of the American Medical Association, 185*, 94-101.

Lalive d'Epinay, C. (2004). Les dernières années de longues vies. L'incapacité lourde constitue-t-elle aujourd'hui la dernière étape de la vie? [The last years of a long life. Does severe disability now make up life's last lap?]. *Gérontologie et Société, 110*, 121-129.

Rockwood, K. (1997). Medical management of frailty: Confessions of a gnostic. *Canadian Medical Association Journal*(157), 1081-1084.

Speechley, M., & Tinetti, M. E. (1991). Falls and injuries in frail and vigorous community elderly persons. *Journal of the American Geriatrics Society, 39*, 46-52.

Spini, D., Ghisletta, P., Guilley, E., & Lalive d'Epinay, C. (2007). Frail elderly. In J. E. Birren (Ed.), *Encyclopedia of Gerontology. Age, aging, and the aged* (2nd ed., Vol. 1, pp. 572-579). San Diego: Elsevier, Academic Press.

In: The Closing Chapters of Long Lives
Editors: E. Guilley, Ch. J. Lalive d'Epinay

ISBN: 978-1-60456-971-1

Chapter 3

IS THE FINAL STAGE OF A LONG LIFE ONE OF LONG-TERM ADL-DEPENDENCE?

Edith Guilley* and Christian J. Lalive d'Epinay

ABSTRACT

The objectives of this chapter are to assess the risk in very old age of long-term ADL-dependence (defined as ADL-dependence lasting 12 months or more) prior to death and to determine which factors of social status predispose elders to find themselves in such a situation of dependence. One hundred and seventy-two participants in the Swiss Interdisciplinary Longitudinal Study on the Oldest Old (Swilsoo) were interviewed twice during the years preceding their death. Using a logistic regression, gender, occupational category, age at death, and urban/rural residence were analyzed as potential factors conducive to ending life in a condition of long-term ADL-dependence. The stage of long-term ADL-dependence prior to death was reached by 42.4% of the participants and was more frequent among women and among persons who had been employed in the lower occupational categories. Long-term ADL-dependence is not a natural conclusion to long lives: it is a risk but it is not inevitable.

INTRODUCTION

On a societal level, fear of old age can to a large extent be interpreted as a fear of disability and loss of independence (Stone, 2001). The final years of life in very old age are particularly subject to fear, considering that the probability of severe disability increases with age and with approaching death. In spite of these societal and personal worries, our knowledge of the quality of life in the years before death is very limited. Indeed, only a few studies have examined health status prior to death (e.g. Bortz, 1990; Covinsky, Eng, Lui,

---

* This study was presented at the 58th Annual Scientific Meeting of the Gerontological Society of America, Orlando, FL, USA, in November 2005. Correspondence may be addressed to Edith Guilley, Center for Interdisciplinary Gerontology (CIG), Route de Drize 7, Site Battelle, CH –1227 Carouge, Switzerland; edith.guilley@orange.fr

Sands, & Yaffe, 2003; Guralnik, LaCroix, Branch, Kasl, & Wallace, 1991; Liao, McGee, Kaufman, Cao, & Cooper, 1999; Lunney, Lynn, Foley, Lipson, & Guralnik, 2003). Even fewer have focused specifically on very old populations (Palmore & Burchett (1997), Leveille et al. (1999) and Romoren (2003)). Among the latter, the studies by Leveille et al. (1999) and by Palmore and Burchett (1997) focused primarily on the very last interview and consequently did not allow any distinction to be made between long-term ADL-dependence and short-term disability. Apart from the study by Romoren (2003) in Norway, all research on health status prior to death has been conducted in the USA.

What is the risk of suffering from long-term ADL-dependence (defined as ADL-dependence lasting 12 months or more) at the end of a long life? Which social status variables make this outcome more likely? This chapter seeks answers to these two questions using data from a sample of very old persons interviewed twice during the years preceding their death, and residing in different settings. The social status variables investigated as potential determinants of mortality with long-term ADL-dependence in later life were gender, occupational status, age at death and urban/rural residence.

Methods

Participants

Participants in the first cohort of the Swiss Interdisciplinary Longitudinal Study on the Oldest Old (Swilsoo) who died between February 1994 and September 2004 are taken into account in this chapter (see chapter 1 for a description of the sample). Deaths recorded in the second cohort were excluded for two reasons. In a cohort-specific analysis, they would have been insufficient in number, and in an analysis combining the two cohorts, they would have introduced a bias in the relationship between mortality with ADL-dependence and age at death. Participants in the second cohort – the more recent – were monitored for five years only (*versus* ten years for the first cohort), implying an arbitrary lower age at death in the second cohort compared with the first one.

Because the aim was to analyze long-term (i.e. lasting 12 months or more) ADL-dependence prior to death, the analytical sample was restricted to the 172 persons (out of the total of 243 decedents) who were interviewed twice before death (participants being interviewed every 12 or 18 months). The social status characteristics of the analytical sample closely matched those of the other deceased participants except that the latter were younger. The analytical sample consisted of 82 women (47.7% of the sample) and 90 men; 47.1% were residents of the urban area, 24.0% were of middle or upper class, 35.0% had been self-employed, 12.9% white-collar workers and 28.1% blue-collar workers. The mean age at death was 87.5 (+/-2.5) years.

Health Measures

ADL-dependence was defined as the need for help from another person in performing at least one of five activities of daily living (washing, dressing and undressing, eating, rising from and going to bed, and moving from one room to another; cf. Katz, Ford, Moskowitz, Jackson, & Jaffee, 1963). Across the study waves, the five items reached on average a reliability level (Cronbach's alpha) of 0.90. ADL-dependence was shown to have predictive validity for admission to skilled-nursing facilities and mortality (Gill, Robison, & Tinetti, 1998). In this paper we analyze long-term ADL-dependence prior to death, defined as ADL-dependence lasting 12 months or more. More precisely, pre-mortem long-term ADL-dependence was recorded for people who reported ADL-dependence at two successive waves of data collection immediately preceding death. Considering that recovery from ADL-dependence is a rare occurrence just prior to death, the fifteen individuals who reported ADL-dependence at the last wave prior to death and for whom death occurred twelve months or more after the last interview were also considered to be suffering from long-term ADL-dependence.

Social Status Variables

The social status variables used in the present study include geographical area of residence (urban or semi-rural), gender, age at death and former occupational category (small self-employed persons – smallholders and owners of small businesses - blue-collar workers, white-collar workers, middle or upper social classes – including liberal professions). The occupational categorization was based on the main occupation held during the subject's working life. A household classification was used whereby each individual was classified according to the "higher" of the two spouses' respective social rankings. This classification is an adapted version of the six-category class schema presented by Desrosières and Thévenot (1992).

Analysis Strategies

We assessed the risk of long-term ADL-dependence prior to death in very old age according to social status factors by conducting univariate descriptive analyses and then a multivariate logistic regression. The multivariate logistic regression analyzed the risk of long-term ADL-dependence prior to death as a function of gender, occupational category, age at death and geographical area of residence. Also examined were interaction effects between the above-mentioned factors, but no significant interactions were found. The logistic regression model was fitted using SPSS 13 (SPSS Inc., 1990). Some of the subjects lived longer and consequently participated in the study for a longer time than others. As a consequence, we might have found longer periods of ADL-dependence for the former just because they were observed for longer. To avoid this bias, we sought to determine which social status factors influenced the probability of long-term ADL-dependence instead of analyzing the duration of ADL-dependence per se.

Table 1. Percentage of long-term ADL-dependent persons among decedents, by social status variables

	Percentage long-term ADL-dependent (n=172)	p-value[1]
Total sample	42.4	
Age at death		
≤ 87.5 years	39.7	.073
> 87.5 years	60.3	
Gender		
Male	42.5	.026
Female	57.5	
Geographical area		
Semi-rural	64.4	.010
Urban	35.6	
Occupational category		
Middle/upper	9.6	<.001
White-collar workers	8.2	
Blue-collar workers	34.2	
Small self-employed	47.9	

[1] p values are based on chi-square analysis.

RESULTS

The percentage of long-term ADL-dependence among decedents is shown in Table 1 by social status variables according to univariate analyses. Forty-two percent (n = 73/172) of the participants died after a long period of ADL-dependence. Those who were long-term ADL-dependent were more likely to be female, and to live in the semi-rural area. Differences in the risk of long-term ADL-dependence by occupational category were pronounced: the risk was highest among the small self-employed, followed by blue-collar workers and white-collar workers, while persons from the middle or upper classes presented the lowest risk of long-term ADL-dependence.

Table 2. Multivariate logistic regression analysis of social status determinants of long-term ADL-dependence prior to death (n = 172)

	Odd Ratio	95% C.I.	p-value
Age at death (in years)	1.00	0.87-1.14	0.954
Gender (women)	2.15	1.08-4.30	0.030
Geographical area (urban)	0.61	0.31-1.21	0.159
Middle/upper classes vs blue-collar workers	0.22	0.08-0.61	0.004
White-collar workers vs blue-collar workers	0.29	0.09-0.92	0.036
Small self-employed vs blue-collar workers	1.17	0.53-2.59	0.696

Table 2 shows the results of a multivariate logistic regression evaluating which social status factors predispose elders to suffer from long-term ADL-dependence before the end of life. Such dependence was more frequent among women, and was less likely among persons of the middle and upper classes and among white-collar workers. Women were about twice as likely as men to be long-term ADL-dependent. Persons from the middle and upper classes and white-collar workers were three to four times less likely than blue-collar workers to be long-term ADL-dependent.

DISCUSSION

This study was prompted by two questions: (1) what is the risk of suffering from long-term ADL-dependence at the end of a long life; and (2) is this risk equally distributed among the social status categories? In the present study, 42.4% of the participants died after suffering from long-term ADL-dependence. This indicates that long-term ADL-dependence is not an inevitable stage in a long life. Our findings are in keeping with the few existing studies on the final years of very long lives, which indicate that a majority of people aged over 80 years die without having suffered from any serious dementia or severe dependence (Leveille et al., 1999; Palmore & Burchett, 1997; Romoren, 2003). However, these encouraging results need to be put into perspective. Indeed, a non-chronically disabled older person is not necessarily a person without health problems. Additional analysis of Swilsoo data showed that less than 15% of the participants were robust (i.e. they had deficiencies in one or more of the domains of mobility, memory, energy and physical or sensory capacity) through most of the last years of their lives (Guilley, Armi, Ghisletta, & Lalive d'Epinay, 2008).

While the evolution of health during the life course is known to depend on gender (e. g. Lahelma, Arber, Martikainen, Rahkonen, & Silventoinen, 2001), little research has been done on this gender difference in the final years of life, particularly on samples of the oldest old living in contrasting residential settings. Our finding was that, even controlling for age at death and socio-occupational category, women are more likely to go through a long period of ADL dependence. This bears out the paradox that, although women tend to live longer lives than men, they are more likely to experience long-term ADL-dependence. One explanation suggested by Romoren (2003) is that women may survive better under ADL-dependence than men, while the higher mortality among men may rescue many of them from a later period of ADL-dependence. Additional research should determine whether different diseases are responsible for gender differences in the quality of the last years of life. It may be that more men die a sudden death without going through a lengthy period of ADL-dependence.

It is well established (e.g. Land & Yang, 2006) that health in adulthood is affected by social inequalities but there is less unanimity about the effect of such inequalities in later life. Some studies have revealed a dwindling effect on health while others have pointed to an unchanged or increasing effect (e.g. Ferraro & Farmer, 1996a). The dwindling effect of inequalities in later life is often a matter of selective survival (Ferraro & Farmer, 1996b), while the increasing effect is in line with the cumulative disadvantage theory (Dannefer, 2003). The present paper demonstrates that, in spite of the differential mortality, membership of an occupational category does have consequences for health in very old age, even up to the years prior to death: former self-employed persons and blue-collar workers have a higher risk than the other occupational categories of ending life in a state of long-term ADL-dependence. This finding fails to support the hypothesis that health disparities of social origin tend to disappear at the end of long lives. The unfavorable working conditions of lower social classes, their behavioral risk factors such as less healthy nutrition, their psychosocial disadvantages including the feeling of having little control over one's own life generally, and unequal access to care and treatment (c.f. Land & Yang, 2006) may be at the root of ADL-dependence prior to death. Another conclusion to be drawn from Swilsoo data is that individuals from a lower occupational category experience a greater functional decline during the years prior to death compared to those from higher occupational categories (Guilley & Lalive d'Epinay, 2008).

In the present study, we found that the risk of long-term ADL-dependence before dying was similar for the oldest decedents as for those of their contemporaries who had already died. Thus a longer life was not necessarily burdened by a greater risk of long-term ADL-dependence. This finding runs counter to the results reported by Guralnik et al. (1991), who showed that the probability of having ADL disabilities increased with a longer life span for persons aged 65 and over, and by Romoren (2003), who arrived at a parallel conclusion for long-term ADL dependence in a sample of the oldest old. The disparity may stem from the longer monitoring period of these studies compared to Swilsoo (more than 10 years versus 10 years). Another explanation for our finding that ADL-dependence did not increase with greater age at death may lie in the fitness of the Swiss and their propensity for hiking.

Our data also showed that the risk of long-term ADL-dependence was greater among the rural population than among the urban dwellers. This difference is primarily a reflection of the occupational structure in each region, a fact that we confirmed by controlling for occupational category in our multivariate analysis (Table 2). Elders who had previously done manual work, in industry or as smallholders for example, were more likely to live in the semi-rural area ($\chi^2 = 23.0$; $p < .001$). This finding is in line with that of Palmore & Burchett (1997), who, to our knowledge, are the only researchers to have considered the effect of geographical area on the risk of disability in the final years of life.

The feature of this paper is that it highlights a sample of the oldest old in the final stage of life, a subject on which little work has been done. Also, the design of Swilsoo was such that subjects living in different residential environments, including institutions, could be observed over a lengthy time period. Three limitations must however be mentioned. First, the design and stratification of our study brought about an overrepresentation of men, community-dwelling persons and the rural elderly in our sample of decedents. However, this did not affect our analysis of the way in which social status variables impinge upon long-term ADL-dependence prior to death. Second, our decision to work through proxies when necessary may have had a bearing on our results. Proxies were, however, expected to report on facts rather than feelings or opinions, a method of evaluation considered by Epstein, Hall, Tognetti, Son, & Conant (1989) to be fairly reliable. Third, the percentage of decedents dying after long-term ADL-dependence changed according to whether participants classified as ADL-dependent at wave t were considered dependent the day after wave t-1 or the day before wave t. Checking the results obtained by applying different definitions of long-term ADL-dependence, we found that the percentage of persons dying after long-term ADL-dependence varied from 34 to 53%. Here again, however, the effect of the social status variables remained unchanged whatever the definition adopted.

This study demonstrates how questionable it is to see the years prior to death as a time of long-term ADL-dependence. Nowadays, the terminal stage of a long life is not inevitably one of ADL-dependence: it is a risk, but not an ineluctable occurrence. The degree of risk varies according to gender and occupational category. The fact that the findings of two studies, one relating to Switzerland and the other to a coastal town in Norway (Romoren, 2003) with rather different occupational contexts, are consistent with one other boosts confidence in the conclusions concerning the determinants of long-term ADL-dependence prior to death. Further research is, however, needed to determine which social or psychological factors may prevent ante-mortem ADL-dependence.

References

Bortz, W. M. (1990). The trajectory of dying. Functional status in the last year of life. *Journal of the American Geriatrics Society, 38*, 146-150.

Covinsky, K. E., Eng, C., Lui, L.-Y., Sands, L. P., & Yaffe, K. (2003). The last 2 years of life: Functional trajectories of frail older people. *Journal of the American Geriatrics Society, 51*, 492-498.

Dannefer, D. (2003). Cumulative advantage/disadvantage and the life course: Cross-fertilizing age and social science theory. *Journal of Gerontology: Social Sciences, 58B*(6), S327-S337.

Desrosières, A., & Thévenot, L. (1992). *Les Catégories Socio-Professionnelles [The Occupational Categories]*. Paris: La Découverte.

Epstein, A. M., Hall, J. A., Tognetti, J., Son, L. H., & Conant, L. (1989). Using proxies to evaluate quality of life. *Medical Care, 27*, 91-98.

Ferraro, K. F., & Farmer, M. M. (1996a). Double jeopardy to health hypothesis for African Americans: Analysis and critique. *Journal of Health and Social Behavior, 37*(1), 27-43.

Ferraro, K. F., & Farmer, M. M. (1996b). Double jeopardy, aging as leveler, or persistent health inequality? A longitudinal analysis of white and black Americans. *Journal of Gerontology: Social Sciences, 51B*, S319-S328.

Gill, T. M., Robison, J. T., & Tinetti, M. E. (1998). Difficulty and dependence: Two components of the disability continuum among community-living older persons. *Annals of Internal Medicine, 128*(2), 96-101.

Guilley, E., Armi, F., Ghisletta, P., & Lalive d'Epinay, C. (2008). Trajectoires de vie, transitions de santé [Life trajectories, health transitions]. In C. Lalive d'Epinay, & D. Spini (Eds.), *Les Années Fragiles: la Vie au-delà de 80 ans* (pp. 123-142). Québec, Canada: Les Presses de l'Université de Laval.

Guilley, E., & Lalive d'Epinay, C. (2008). Social status and mortality with activity of daily living disability in later life. *Journal of Gerontology: Social Sciences, 63*(3), 192-196.

Guralnik, J. M., LaCroix, A. Z., Branch, L. G., Kasl, S. V., & Wallace, R. B. (1991). Morbidity and disability in older persons in the years prior to death. *American journal of public health, 81*(4), 443-447.

Katz, S., Ford, A. B., Moskowitz, R. W., Jackson, B. A., & Jaffee, M. W. (1963). Studies of illness in the aged. The index of ADL: a standardized measure of biological and psychosocial function. *Journal of the American Medical Association, 185*, 94-101.

Lahelma, E., Arber, S., Martikainen, P., Rahkonen, O., & Silventoinen, K. (2001). The myth of gender differences in health: Social structural determinants across adult ages in Britain and Finland. *Current Sociology, 49*(3), 31-54.

Land, K. C., & Yang, Y. (2006). Morbidity, disability, and mortality. In R. H. Binstock, & L. K. George (Eds.), *Handbook of Aging and the Social Sciences* (6th ed., pp. 41-58). San Diego, California: Academic Press.

Leveille, S. G., Guralnik, J. M., Ferrucci, L., & Langlois, J. A. (1999). Aging successfully until death in old age: opportunities for increasing active life expectancy. *American Journal of Epidemiology, 149*(7), 654-664.

Liao, Y., McGee, D. L., Kaufman, J. S., Cao, G., & Cooper, R. S. (1999). Socioeconomic status and morbidity in the last years of life. *American Journal of Public Health, 89*(4), 569-572.

Lunney, J. R., Lynn, J., Foley, D. J., Lipson, S., & Guralnik, J. M. (2003). Patterns of functional decline at the end of life. *Journal of the American Medical Association, 289*(18), 2387-2392.

Palmore, E. B., & Burchett, B. M. (1997). Predictors of disability in the final year of life. *Journal of Aging and Health, 9*(3), 283-297.

Romoren, T. I. (2003). *Last Years of Long Lives, the Larvik Study*. London: Routledge.

SPSS Inc. (1990). *SPSS Reference Guide*. Chicago: SPSS International.

Stone, S. D. (2001). Disability, dependence, and old age: Problematic constructions. *Canadian Journal on Aging, 22*(1), 59-67.

PART 2: EVENTS AND CHANGES

In: The Closing Chapters of Long Lives
Editors: E. Guilley, Ch. J. Lalive d'Epinay

ISBN: 978-1-60456-971-1

Chapter 4

SELF-REPORTED CHANGES: RELATION WITH HEALTH, ACTIVITY AND WELL-BEING

Christian J. Lalive d'Epinay**, *Stefano Cavalli and Luc A. Guillet

ABSTRACT

This chapter deals with the awareness of change in the course of very old age. The main research questions are: How do elders perceive the dynamic of change in their life? What is its intensity? Which are the main domains of life impinged by changes they consider as important? Are self-reported changes related to "objective" transformations in the fields of health, well-being and activity?

At the end of the first five-year term, 80% of the survivors mentioned important changes in their life, the mean number of changes being three. After 10 years, the proportion rose to 88%, with six changes as a mean. The chief domains of change were health and family (83% of the changes). When another person was involved in the change, he/she was almost always a close relative (94%) and the major event was bereavement (47%). Self-reported bereavements and health problems were associated with a significant decline in the elders' well-being; those reporting a deterioration in health did in fact undergo a serious health decline, both physical and functional, and a reduction of activities.

* Correspondence concerning this chapter should be addressed to Christian J. Lalive d'Epinay, Center for Interdisciplinary Gerontology, Route de Drize 7, Site Battelle, CH – 1227 Carouge, Switzerland; Christian.Lalive@socio.unige.ch

THEORETICAL BACKGROUND

Transitions, Life Events, and Turning Points

In the literature on the life course and human development, significant change is most often associated with the notions of transition, life event, and turning point. Although in common use, these notions lack consensual definitions: the life course perspective often refers to transitions and turning points, research on stress to life events. Each of these three notions has connotations of change, but the kind of change involved in each seems to differ.

In the case of transitions, life course researchers point at the major periods of change across individual life courses (Chirboga, 1995; Hägestad, 1990). A transition is « usually tied to the acquisition or relinquishment of roles » (Elder, 1998; Schulenberg, Maggs, & O'Malley, 2003; Settersten, 1999), and may involve a change in terms of identity (Glaser & Strauss, 1971). Transitions are mainly seen as normal changes occurring during the development of human life, some of them being normative in the sense that they are organized and regulated by society (Cain, 1964; Mayer & Schoepflin, 1989).

Transitions and life events both refer to changes in an individual's state. A transition is often seen as a gradual change related to exit from or entry into a role, whereas an event is usually conceptualized as a relatively abrupt change (Elder, 1985, 1998; Settersten, 1999). Life events can be defined as objective changes « that disrupt or threaten to disrupt the individual's usual activities » (Dohrenwned & Dohrenwend, 1969; George, 1995); as a consequence, they induce a need for adjustment (McLeod, 1996). Life events can be construed as markers or causes of transitions (Reese & Smyer, 1983).

A transition or a life event may mark a turning point if it involves a substantial change, either objective or subjective, in the direction of a person's life (Abbott, 1997; Elder, 1998; Rutter, 1996). Historic events – wars, economic crises, etc. – or natural disasters – earthquakes, fires, avalanches, etc. – may disrupt individual life courses and may be perceived as turning points but so may individual events such as a car crash or a severe illness (Hareven & Masaoka, 1988).

Measuring and Categorizing Life Changes

Most empirical research on transitions and, especially, on life events has been based on pre-established checklists and aggregate measures (for an overview, see Settersten, 1999). Criticisms have been leveled at these findings, pinpointing a class, gender, ethnic and age bias in the selection of events, a tendency to over-represent negative and undesirable events, and an inadequate reflection of the multidimensional aspect of the life events (e.g. Reese & Smyer, 1983; Settersten, 1999). Turning points, on the other hand, are mainly approached by means of open-ended questions such as: « Have you ever experienced events or situations which you regarded as turning points in your life? » (Hareven & Masaoka, 1988) or « Looking back, what do you think were the periods of major change, the turning points in your life? » (M. Fiske & Chiriboga, 1990).

Since about 1980, life-span developmental psychology has proposed several taxonomies of life events, which may also be helpful in categorizing changes in general. A classic distinction is made between four main sources of change: biological, social, personal-psychological and physical-environmental (Brim & Ryff, 1980). Reese and Smyer (1983) cross-tabulated these four sources with 14 contexts of life (family, residence, health, work, etc.), thus obtaining a 54-cell grid in which they classified 355 life events founded on a sample of the relevant literature. This taxonomy is based on the conceptual distinction between the origin (or source) of a change and the domains of life affected. But other criteria may be considered, e.g., the likelihood of its occurrence, its reversibility, its link with age or social norms, and its controllability, which is particularly relevant for adults' self-development (Diehl, 1999).

Relation with Health and Everyday Life

Research on life events is based on the assumption that a life event is an acute stressor which forces the individual to adjust his behavior substantially and which can lead to physical and psychological disorders (George, 1995; McLanahan & Sorensen, 1985; McLeod, 1996). Early studies on change as a stressor focused on the hypothesis that any life event is negatively related to health, and that the more an individual experiences such events, the greater are the physical and psychological disturbances (e.g. Brown & Birley, 1968; Dohrenwend & Dohrenwend, 1974). Studies have also shown that some events are better predictors of negative outcomes than total event scores. This implies that events vary in stressfulness because of differences in their characteristics or « traits », such as undesirability, uncontrollability or unpredictability (Wheaton, 1990). For example, undesirable or negative life events are related to psychological distress (for a meta-analysis, see Kraaij, Arensman, & Sopinhoven, 2002) (for some recent longitudinal studies, see Clémence, Karmaniola, Green, & Spini, 2007; A. Fiske, Gatz, & Pedersen, 2003). Mirroring this, some studies have shown that desirable and expected events have a positive impact on well-being (Diehl, 1999; Stallings, Dunham, Gatz, Baker, & Bengtson, 1997).

A number of methodological problems arise in this context. Firstly, the same or very similar items – especially health-related items – may be included in both life-event inventories and dependent variable scales (Thoits, 1981); secondly, an event may cause psychological distress, but the opposite may also be true: some events may be the result of psychological distress or symptoms of depression (Kessler, 1997). The trait approach has also been criticized by researchers who argue that an event cannot be classified unequivocally as undesirable or desirable. Brown and Harris (1978) point out that the meaning of events depends upon the context in which they occur and varies from person to person according to the individual's resources or coping strategy (see also McLeod & Kessler, 1990).

Human development continues from birth to death and all life periods involve unique and important developmental experiences (P. B. Baltes, Lindenberger, & Staudinger, 1998). Three trends are said to be associated with the advance into old age, one related to the frequency of the life changes occurring, the second to the domain of life they impact, and the third to their valence. The number of events occurring seems to dwindle in old age (M. Fiske & Chiriboga, 1990; Goldberg & Comstock, 1980; McLanahan & Sorensen, 1985). It has been argued that this observation is a result of methodological bias; the age difference in number of life events may be induced by the content of the checklists used, which tend to over-represent events that are relevant to young people (McLeod, 1996); furthermore, research on changes across the life course rarely includes the oldest-old, and the generalization of results obtained on the basis of younger samples seems questionable. Two more recent studies on the entire adult life span have shown that life is at its most eventful during the first stage of adult life, but the intensity of events remains at the same level from about mid-life to the end (Cavalli et al., 2006; Chirboga, 1997). According to the first of these studies, as old age advances there is no decrease in the frequency of events but a growing concentration in a few domains of life (see also Cavalli & Lalive d'Epinay, in press), which is explained (a) by the narrowed scope of the elders' role (Aldwin & Levenson, 2001), and (b) by increasing frailty and health problems (Folkman, Lazarus, Pimley, & Novacek, 1987). The balance between desirable and undesirable changes, gains and losses, becomes slowly negative, with uncompensated losses growing in weight (P. B. Baltes & Smith, 1999; Heckhausen, Dixon, & Baltes, 1989). Gender differences observed are related to the respective social roles: women quote more changes related to family and health, men to their profession and finance (M. Fiske & Chiriboga, 1990); but no specific information about old age is to be found.

Research has also shown that, even if many of the life changes experienced in later life consist of losses, most older people cope fairly effectively with them (Ferraro, 2001). Losses induce adaptive strategies of selection rather than prompting an automatic decline in health and effective functioning (M. M. Baltes & Carstensen, 1996). In addition, this ability to adapt to changes has a positive impact on the well-being of the older people (Johnson & Barer, 1993).

Research Questions

This paper deals with the recent important changes in life reported by a sample of the oldest old. The approach is thus subjective, centering on the awareness that the elders have of the dynamic of change operating at that stage of their life. Because of the lack of research on this topic, our study was exploratory in nature, and we proceeded by means of research questions rather than with well-established hypotheses. Our main concerns were:

1. Intensity: the frequency of perceived changes.
2. Domains: the classification of the changes. What are the main categories of self-reported changes in very old age?
3. Persons: did the reported change impinge directly on the elder, or indirectly via another person or persons close to him/her?
4. Changes and events: are self-reported changes always linked to an identified event? If not, what kinds of « uneventful » changes are mentioned?
5. Relation between specified categories of perceived changes and the evolution of health (physical and functional), well-being and activities.
6. Gender differences: in studying the above five concerns, do we observe gender specificities?

METHODS[1]

Data and Respondents

From the second Swilsoo wave onward, the interviewer's trigger question was: *"Since our last visit, has any important change occurred in your life?"*. When changes were reported, the interviewer asked for a description of each change and an accurate indication of the time of occurrence.

The word "change" was chosen because it is generic, a component of the three related concepts of transition, life event and turning point. By asking about important changes, we focused on those changes that in the respondents' opinion had had an impact on their lives. "Since our last visit" refers to the time lapse of 12 to 18 months between two waves of interviews. Being subjective in nature, this question was asked only at the beginning of face-to-face interviews with the older persons themselves. Altogether, this paper is based on 652 individuals at baseline; the 2,496 questionnaires gathered constituting the raw material for our analyses.

Measures

Perceived Life Changes

The answers to the trigger question were coded according to the number of changes, the mention or absence of mention of an identified event, the person mainly concerned, and the domain of life affected by the change (adapted and simplified from Reese & Smyer, 1983).

Health, Well-being and Activities

We distinguished two dimensions of health status:

Physical pains. This question listed a number of parts of the body which may cause suffering (see Lalive d'Epinay, Bickel, Maystre, & Vollenwyder, 2000). Eleven items were proposed: lower limbs, upper limbs, head/face, back, heart, respiratory organs, stomach/abdomen, genital/urinary organs, chest, fever, other. For each part of the body, the respondent reported the degree of his or her suffering on a three-point scale: no suffering at all, some suffering, great suffering (for a similar measure, see Kane, Bell, Riegler, Wilson, & Kane, 1993). By taking only the last answer into account and applying it to the 11 possible parts of the body, we arrived at a scale ranging from 0 (no acute suffering) to 11 (11 parts of the body with acute pain). Sample mean at first wave, W_1 (*SD*) = 0.82 (1.16).

Functional health. The individual's ability to accomplish the activities of daily living was assessed. The study covered five basic activities – toileting, eating and cutting up food, dressing and undressing, rising and going to bed, and moving around within the apartment (Katz, Downs, Cash, & Grotz, 1970) – and three measures of mobility – moving around outside, walking at least 200 meters, and going up and down stairs (Rosow & Breslau, 1966). The overall score, ranging from 0 to 16, was the sum of the responses calculated as follows:

[1] For a detailed presentation of Swilsoo's research program and design, see chapter 1.

unable to do alone (2), can do but with difficulty (1), can do easily (0). Sample mean at W_1 (*SD*) = 2.34 (1.26).

Well-being was recorded by means of the Self-Assessing Depression Scale (SADS, see Wang, Treul, & Alverno, 1975), as adapted by Lalive d'Epinay and colleagues (2000). Replies of « never » (0), « rarely » (1), « often » (2) or « always » (3) were recorded for 13 items: feels tired, has trouble sleeping, feels sad, feels lonely, has crying spells or feels like it, feels worried, feels irritable, feels anxious, lacks confidence in the future, lacks appetite, finds time passes slowly, lacks self-confidence, has no pleasure in doing things. This scale ranged from 0 (no symptoms) to 39. Sample mean at W_1 (SD) = 8.13 (6.00).

Activities were measured on the basis of a list of five social activities: playing games (cards, board games, chess, Scrabble), visiting coffees, tea rooms, restaurants, attending religious services, participating in trips or outings, and attending local fairs or celebrations. The regularity of active participation was measured, starting from a threshold of one activity at least once a month for the first three activities and of at least once a year for the last two. A scale of regular and active participation (ranging from 0 to 5) was constructed. Sample mean at W_1 (*SD*) = 2.12 (1.37).

ANALYSES

In order to study the frequency of changes and their classification, bivariate analyses were mainly used. Multilevel analyses were applied to scrutinize the relation between the perceived changes and the evolution of health, well-being and activities. Multilevel models were developed for the purpose of analyzing data with multilevel sets (e.g. repeated measures for one individual). They allow the use of repeated measures where both the number of interviews per participant and the time intervals between interviews vary. Furthermore, multilevel analyses can tolerate an incomplete data set because they use all available data instead of restricting the analysis to individuals who participated in all nine waves, thus limiting the selectivity effects (Bryk & Raudenbush, 1992).

A model was tested for each of the four dependent variables (physical pains, functional health, well-being and activities). Age (centered on its grand mean), the category of change (see below) and the measure of health, well-being or activities at the previous wave (W_{n-1}) were included as level-1, time-varying predictors; gender and cohorts as a level-2, time-invariant predictor. Because cohort analyses revealed no cohort effect, we merged the two cohorts into a unique analysis. Also examined were the possible interaction effects between gender and the categories of change. Results were reported with a robust estimation of the standard errors and the effects were tested by the method of restricted maximum likelihood using HLM version 6.0 (Raudenbush, Bryk, Cheong, & Congdon, 2004).

Analyzing the relation between perceived changes and the evolution of domains of the elders' life raises problems of both a conceptual (which changes or events must be taken in account?) and a methodological nature (what is the nature of the link: covariate or causal?). There is now a consensus that changes (or events) constitute a very heterogeneous category and that different kinds of change may have different consequences. Furthermore, the same kind of event can be subjectively lived in opposite ways, depending on the general context of occurrence. In our study, most of the reported health changes were seen as deteriorations but in some cases the elder pointed to an improvement; moving to a nursing home can be seen as a relief or as a loss. Family events were clearly divided into two groups, weddings and births being seen as happy events, and bereavements and divorces as sad ones having the effect of shrinking the elder's family network. Thus, as a first step, it was necessary to assign to a given category only changes of the same nature and with the same valence. Then, we had to set aside all the sequences where an elder mentioned two or more changes different in nature or contradictory in valence (for example, a wedding and a bereavement or a health problem and a birth in the family).

In the end, we kept only the following three categories: *health trouble changes* – elders reporting negative health changes (n = 338); *bereavements* (n = 93); and *positive changes* – i.e. all the changes mentioned as positive (half of them being family events and the others referring to health improvement, etc.) (n = 73). Because of the scan number, the positive change category could not be split according to domain and it therefore remained heterogeneous. As control group, we used the *no change* sequences (n = 1113).

To summarize, applying multilevel analyses, we established whether the health, well-being and activities of elders reporting the occurrence of a specified change between W_{n-1} and W_n evolved in a significantly different way to the health, well-being and activities of elders reporting no change for the period in question. The direction of the evolution was established by comparing the means of the dependent variables of the three categories of perceived changes in W_{n-1} and W_n.

Table 1. Proportion of elders reporting changes, per five-year period, among all participants and among survivors, with indication of number of changes reported and mean number of changes per respondent among those reporting change

	First five-year term (w2-w5) Two cohorts		Second five-year term (w6-w9) First cohort		Ten-year term (w2-w9) First cohort	
	All participants	Survivors[1]	All participants	Survivors[1]	All participants	Survivors[1]
Number of elders	498	283	105	49	234	49
Percentage of elders mentioning changes	68.3	80.2	73.3	81.6	74.4	87.8
Mean[2]	2.8	3.0	2.5	3.1	3.7	5.9
Number of changes	952	680	194	125	644	254

[1] Participants at the last wave = [respondents at wave 2 – (dropouts + deceased)].
[2] Mean number of changes among those mentioning a change.

RESULTS

Frequency of Perceived Changes

At the end of the first five-year term, 68% of the elders in both cohorts taken as a whole reported changes, the mean number of changes being slightly less than three (table 1). Among the survivors, the proportion was 80%, with a mean of three changes. After the second five-year term, very similar results were recorded. At the end of the 10-year period, three quarters of the respondents (first cohort) mentioned changes, with four as a mean, and 88 percent of the survivors, with a mean of six changes. No link was observed between the duration of the inter-wave period (12 or 18 months), and the proportion of elders mentioning a change.

Domain and Subject of the Changes

In table 2 the changes are classified by domain of life – according to a simplified version of Reese and Smyer's (1983) taxonomy – and the first subject of the change (ego versus alter). According to the elders, the overriding element in the dynamic of change at their age is health: two-thirds of all the mentions pointed at health, mainly health problems and declines. Ninety percent of the mentions concerning health referred to the elder him/herself, while the remaining 10% pointed at a close relative. Second, but far behind with 17% of the mentions, come family events in the form of life passages. Among them, the last passage is the most frequently seen as the source of an important change: 64% of the family events reported were bereavements. The third and fourth categories, spatial changes and activities, accounted for only 6% and 5% of the mentions respectively, leaving a remainder of 6%. For the very old, the significant changes affecting their life mainly involve health and/or family.

About a quarter of the reported changes did not impinge directly on the elder but on a person close to him or her. With few exceptions, the alter was a very close relative, usually the spouse (or the life companion) in the case of health (76%), or descendants in the case of births and weddings (98%). A noteworthy sidelight is that two elders proudly mentioned their own wedding, one at the age of 85 and the other at 87. Among the bereavements, 87% referred to family members. Against a background of 136 mentions of death (spouse 26%, sibling 24% , children or grandchildren 12%, other relative 24%), 41 of births and 14 of weddings, the elders seemed to more affected by the loss of a loved one than by the arrival of offspring in the family.

Event-related versus Non-event-related Changes

At each wave, the proportion of perceived changes not related to an objective event ranged from 12% to 23%; altogether, 19% were not event-related. As table 3 shows, the typical feature of these gradual changes is that they almost always (87%) referred to the elders' health. Actually, one quarter of the health changes were not linked to any specific event such as an illness, a fall, hospitalization or an operation. Often, the respondents spoke of an insidious underlying process and had no clear idea about its cause other than seeing in it a fatalistic connection with age. Table 4 gives some examples of non-event-related changes.

Relation with Health, Well-being and Activities

Are the subjectively quoted « important changes in life » associated with objective changes (objective meaning that they could be measured by standardized scales introduced in the questionnaire) in health (physical and functional) or well-being of the elders, or in the range of their activities? We consider here three categories of change – ego health troubles, bereavements, and positive changes – with the no-change sequences as control group.

Table 2. Classification of perceived changes by subject of change and domain of life (W_2-W_9)

	Subject of change					
Domain	Ego		Alter		Total	
	n	%	n	%	n	%
Health	674	80	76	26	750	66
Family events	16	2	184	63	200	17
Births	-		*41*		*41*	
Weddings	*2*		*14*		*16*	
Deaths	-		*118*		*118*	
Other	*14*		*11*		*25*	
Spatial	53	6	11	4	64	6
Institutionalization	*25*		*6*		*31*	
Other	*28*		*5*		*33*	
Activities	53	6	0		53	5
Other	53	6	21	7	74	6
Self	*15*		*0*		*15*	
Everyday life	*13*		*0*		*13*	
Finances	*6*		*0*		*6*	
Death of friends	-		*18*		*18*	
Miscellaneous	*19*		*3*		*22*	
Total	849	100	292	100	1141	100
%		74		26		100

Table 3. Event-related and non-event-related changes by domain of life (W_2-W_9)

	Event		No event		Total	
Domain	n	%	n	%	n	%
Health	558	60	192	87	750	65
Other	367	40	29	13	396	35
Total	925	100	221	100	1146	100

$\chi^2 = 55.617, p < .001$.

Table 4. Examples of non-event-related changes: health-related and other

Domain	Examples of answers
Health (n = 192)	- « My eyesight has worsened and I don't feel so strong » - « I am less mobile than I used to be » - « I feel listless » - « I am failing little by little » - « I feel my age » - « I am going downhill generally » - « I don't hear so well now » - « I have no strength left and I tire easily » - « I haven't the same pep as before » - « I am not what I used to be » - « I am gradually beginning to talk nonsense! » - « I am getting weak in the legs »
Other (n = 29)	- « I work a little bit less » - « I have a quieter life with less work » - « I do not visit as often as before I went into the nursing home » - « Financially, my resources are running low » - « Human beings are becoming more and more dehumanized » - « Where is poetry today? Science and robots worry me »

Table 5. Self-reported negative health changes, bereavements and positive changes: associations with physical and functional health, depressive symptoms, and activities (multilevel analysis)

	Negative health changes (*vs* no change) n=338		Bereavements (*vs* no change) n=93		Positive changes (*vs* no change) n=73	
	Coeff.	*p value*	*Coeff.*	*p value*	*Coeff.*	*p value*
Physical pains	0.34	<0.001	0.18	0.231	0.13	0.505
Functional disabilities	1.16	<0.001	-0.02	0.916	0.34	0.226
Depressive symptoms	1.26	<0.001	1.30	0.007**	0.53	0.230
Activities	-0.09	0.005	0.03	0.488	0.04	0.414

Note: Age and sex are controlled. No change: n = 1113. Physical pains: scale ranging from 0 (no acute suffering) to 11 (11 parts of the body with acute pain). Functional health: scale ranging from 0 (no disability or difficulty) to 16 (8 disabilities). Well-being: scale ranging from 0 (no depressive symptoms) to 39 (13 frequent depressive symptoms). Social activities: between 0 and 5 regular activities.

The scores on the two dimensions of health, as on well-being and activities, were significantly less favorable for elders reporting serious health problems than for the control group. Analysis of the evolution of means between Wn-1 and Wn showed that the scores of the control group remained stable for all indicators. Further, reporting significant health problems was associated with an increase in physical pains (from 0.90 at Wn-1 to 1.10 at Wn), a rise in functional impairment (from 1.73 to 2.88), an increase in depressive symptoms (from a score of 8.49 to 9.06) and a reduction in activities (from 2.28 to 1.20).

The physical and functional health of the bereaved elders, like their participation in social activities, did not evolve differently from the control group. However, their well-being evolved negatively (from a score of depressive symptoms of 8.14 to 8.98), while in the control group it remained stable. No significant difference was observed between the group reporting a positive change and the control group.

Gender Comparison

All multilevel analyses applied to scrutinize the relation between the perceived changes and the evolution of health, well-being and activities, were controlled by gender. In addition, we systematically tested interactions between gender and categories of change. Analyses split by gender did not reveal any differences between men and women concerning the frequency of perceived changes, their classification, or their relation to an identified event. The only significant interaction was between gender and physical health (Coeff.= -0.55; p-value=0.036*). The physical health of women reporting a positive change evolved more favorably than that of women in the control group, but this was not observed among men.

DISCUSSION

Let us now summarize and discuss the answers that this study provided to our questions.

(1) *Intensity of the change dynamic*. After five years, about 70% of the participants and 80% of the survivors reported important changes, the mean number of changes being three. After 10 years, close to 90 percent of the survivors reported changes, with a mean number of six. Experiencing significant life changes during advanced old age seems to be a widely shared experience. But the perception and intensity vary greatly from one elder to the other: after five years, 30% of the survivors reported one single change and 20% five changes or more. At the end of the 10-year period, 12% mentioned one change, and 19% 10 changes or more. But it must also be said that one in five survivors after five years, and one in ten at the end of the decade, did not report a single significant change; elders of this minority group perceived their current life as a smooth-running process even though, according to other sections of the questionnaire, their life had not been at all eventless during the period; all of them had undergone hospitalization, surgery and/or bereavement or had met with an accident but the fact is that they did not report the experience as having introduced a noteworthy change in their life.

Was life during the eighth and ninth decades of age changing at a faster or slower pace than during the preceding stages? As stated above (see theoretical background), it is often conjectured that the intensity of change peaks during the transition from adolescence to the first stage of adulthood and then tends to decline with age, but the only available research findings with comparable data are those of Cavalli et al. (2006). The authors put the same question on the important changes that had occurred in the respondent's life during the past

12 months to a sample of 622 persons equally divided into five age-groups (20-24, 35-39, 50-54, 65-69, 80-84). According to this study, the stage of entry into adulthood is the most eventful, then a decline is observed up to mid-life (50-54 years). From that time to advanced old age, however, the proportion of persons reporting a change and the density of changes remain constant. Thus life seems to be as eventful during old age as it is during the three preceding decades (see also Cavalli & Lalive d'Epinay, in press).

(2, 3) *Domains of change and persons involved.* The significant self-reported changes in the course of advanced old age display two main features. First, health and family are seen by the elders as the two domains of life which yield the great majority (83%) of the changes, with health coming first and foremost. Second, when an elder is indirectly impinged (27% of the cases), it means, with very few exceptions, that something (good or bad, but more often bad than good) has happened to a close relative (table 2). To our understanding, this does not imply that friendship loses its significance with advancing old age. Later in the questionnaire, when the relational life of the elders was under scrutiny, 177 mentions of the death of a friend were recorded; but in answer to the initial trigger question on *important* changes, only 18 of the 136 mentions of bereavement (13%) referred to a friend, and all the others to a family member. What marks a change in the life of a very old person stems mostly from him/herself or from his/her family. The family is seen by the elders as their most essential, vital, existential world. It is thus understandable also that negative events in the family have a greater impact than positive ones: the loss of a loved one was mentioned 118 times, the arrival of a descendant only 41. This imbalance could reflect the fact that the deaths reported pertained to the loss of someone with whom the elder shared part of his/her life, a host of experiences and many memories. In Antonucci and Akiyama's term, such a death means that a loved one has dropped out of the elder's life convoy for ever (Antonucci & Akiyama, 1995).

Summarizing our findings on questions 1 and 2, what seems to be specific to advanced old age is not an uneventful (or less eventful) life, but the concentration of events and changes in very few domains, the first, health, being the most challenging at that stage of life and the second, family, the most relevant from an existential and affective-relational point of view (cf. Cavalli et al., 2006).

(4) *Event-related and non-event-related changes.* In two cases out of ten, no specific event was linked to the change. Here the event was the change itself. With few exceptions (13%), changes of this kind derived from the health of the elder and were described as invisible, ongoing processes affecting also the elder's moral and daily life (tables 3-4). Some studies have shown that other kinds of gradual, non-event-related changes, mainly psychological maturational transformations, prevail at earlier stages of life and are reported as positive (Cavalli et al., 2006; M. Fiske & Chiriboga, 1990). Thus the predominance of insidious health- related changes seems to be the preserve of old age.

(5) *Relation with health, well-being and activities.* The group reporting a deterioration in health did in fact undergo a serious health decline, both physical and functional, and this process was also associated with impaired well-being and a restriction of activities (table 5).

The elders reporting bereavement suffered from a sharp decline in well-being but their physical and functional health did not evolve differently from the control group. This calls into question the claim that the loss of a close relative affects the health of the bereaved person (for the loss of a child Arbuckle & de Vries, 1995; of a sibling Brubacker, 1992; of a spouse, see Tudiver, Hilditch, Permaul, & McKendree, 1992), but there is no consensus on this topic. Some authors argue that the oldest old develop an ability to cope with negative events and speak of their « aura of survivorship » (Johnson & Barer, 1993; Pearlin, 1994). Nevertheless, the link between self-reported bereavement and decline in well-being suggests that their ability to cope has its limits.

Are the statistically significant relations detected here causal in nature? At the methodological level, the drawback of the model applied here is that it tests whether the group reporting a specified change evolved differently or not from the control group during the same time period according to a given variable. However, we still do not know which of the two changes occurred first. Within this constraint, what conclusions can be drawn?

Firstly, elders proved to have a fairly clear understanding of their evolving health condition and showed the ability to distinguish between benign health troubles and problems of a more serious nature. The group reporting health troubles and the control group both had health problems of various kinds, but the physical and functional health of the former was declining more steeply. It seems justifiable to conclude that this had an adverse effect on their well-being as well as on the organization of their everyday life.

Secondly, the same argument seems to hold true for those who reported that the death of a loved one had changed their life. Both the bereaved and the control group suffered from the loss of family members, but the well-being of the former was strongly affected while no change in well-being was observed among the latter.

(6) *Gender*. No significant gender differences were observed in the frequency of the perceived changes, their classification, or their relation to an identified event. The fact that, at this age, women and men react in the same way may be related to their exit from public and professional life, combined with their existential experience of the frailty process (Spini, Ghisletta, Guilley, & Lalive d'Epinay, 2007).

The only detected gender difference related to women reporting positive change: their physical health had improved and evolved more favorably than among women of the control group. Do older women react more positively than men to happy events? The difference was only slight and it must be remembered that the small number of positive change sequences and the composite character of this category rule out any possibility of drawing conclusions as to its implications with regard to the various domains of life.

CONCLUSION

Life in advanced old age seems to be as eventful as during the preceding decades, but the changes the elders report as significant are concentrated in two domains of life: health and the family circle. The first cause of change – the elders' own health, with 60% of the mentions – stems from the fact that they are growing old, very old. According to most respondents, this simple fact is sufficient to set the impetus of their life along a declining path. Here, our results illustrate the subjective experience of the frailty process.

Going back to Brim and Ryff 's (1980) classification of the sources of change (biological, social, personal-psychological and physical-environmental), biological life is now seen by the elders as the predominant source, not only their own biological life but also the life of their significant others. We have seen that, when a self-reported change impinges on another person, it is almost always a close relative. Let us now add that the event in question is biological in nature in 80% of the cases (health: 26%; deaths: 40%; births: 14%; cf. table 2).

Family events often mark a change in the elders' life but a striking fact is that they report three times more frequently the loss of a loved one than the arrival of an offspring. Both events have strong symbolic meanings. The former ends a partnership, a shared chapter of life, and in a way foreshadows the elder's own death. The latter conveys a feeling of continuity: the person's own life is coming to an end but life goes on, not just some kind of anonymous life but one in which a mysterious part of the elder's own life will survive, the "flesh of my flesh", as a sign of immortality. Why does the first kind of family event take on more importance than the second in the eyes of the elders? The answer could be that the death of a loved one has not only symbolic meanings but also very practical consequences: it marks the end of a relationship, often also the end of exchanges, interactions, visits, forms of support.

Our study focused on the perception that octogenarians have of the changes affecting their life. The approach was subjective in nature. The elders' answers were autobiographical, offering a vivid account of the advanced stage of the aging process in which health problems and the loss of loved ones are a feature. Their testimony demonstrates their keen awareness and acceptance of the true challenges of the last stage of life.

References

Abbott, A. (1997). On the concept of turning point. *Comparative Social Research, 16*, 85-105.

Aldwin, C., & Levenson, M. R. (2001). Stress, coping, and health at mid-life: A developmental perspective. In M. E. Lachman (Ed.), *The handbook of midlife development* (pp. 188-214). New York: Wiley.

Antonucci, T. C., & Akiyama, H. (1995). Convoys of social relations: family and friendships within a life span context. In R. Blieszner, & V. Hilkevitch Bedford (Eds.), *Handbook of aging and the family* (pp. 355-371). London: Greenwood Press.

Arbuckle, N. W., & de Vries, B. (1995). The long-term effects of later life spousal and parental bereavement on personal functioning. *The Gerontologist, 35*, 637-647.

Baltes, M. M., & Carstensen, L. L. (1996). The process of successful ageing. *Ageing and Society, 16*(4), 397-422.

Baltes, P. B., Lindenberger, U., & Staudinger, U. M. (1998). Life-span theory in developmental psychology. In W. Damon, & R. M. Lerner (Eds.), *Handbook of child psychology* (5th ed., Vol. 1: Theoretical models of human development, pp. 1029-1143). New York: Wiley.

Baltes, P. B., & Smith, J. (1999). Multilevel and systemic analyses of old age: Theoretical and empirical evidence for a fourth age. In V. L. Bengtson, & K. W. Schaie (Eds.), *Handbook of Theories of Aging* (pp. 153-173). New York: Springer Publishing Company.

Brim, O. G., & Ryff, C. D. (1980). On the properties of life events. In P. B. Baltes, & O. G. Brim (Eds.), *Life-span development and behavior.* (Vol. 3, pp. 367-388). New York: Academic Press.

Brown, G. W., & Birley, J. L. (1968). Crises and life changes and the onset of schizophrenia. *Journal of Health and Social Behavior, 9*, 203-214.

Brown, G. W., & Haris, T. (1978). *The social origins of depression.* New York: Free Press.

Brubacker, T. (1992). *Later life families*. Beverly Hills: Sage.

Bryk, A. S., & Raudenbush, S. W. (1992). *Hierarchical Linear Models; Applications and data analysis methods*. Newbury Park, CA: Sage Publications.

Cain, L. D. (1964). Life course and social structure. In R. E. Paris (Ed.), *Handbook of modern sociology* (pp. 272-309). Chicago: McNally.

Cavalli, S., Aeby, G., Battistini, M., Borloz, C., Bugnon, G., De Carlo, I., et al. (2006). *Ages de la vie et changements perçus [Stages of life and self-reported changes]*. Genève: Département de sociologie et Centre interfacultaire de gérontologie, Université de Genève.

Cavalli, S., & Lalive d'Epinay, C. (in press). L'identification et l'évaluation des changements au cours de la vie adulte [Identification and evaluation of changes in adulthood]. *Swiss Journal of Sociology, 34*(1).

Chirboga, D. A. (1995). Transitions. In G. L. Maddok (Ed.), *The encyclopedia of aging* (2 ed., pp. 941-942). New York: Springer.

Chirboga, D. A. (1997). In search of continuities and discontinuities across time and culture. In V. L. Bengtson (Ed.), *Adulthood and aging: Research on continuities and discontinuities* (pp. 173-199). New York: Springer.

Clémence, A., Karmaniola, A., Green, E. G., & Spini, D. (2007). Disturbing life events and wellbeing after 80 years of age: A longitudinal comparison of survivors and the deceased over five years. *Ageing and Society, 27*(1), 1-19.

Diehl, M. (1999). Self-development in adulthood and aging: The role of critical life events. In C. D. Ryff, & V. W. Marshall (Eds.), *The self and society in aging processes* (pp. 150-183). New York: Springer.

Dohrenwend, B. S., & Dohrenwend, B. P. (1974). Overview and prospects for research on stressful life events. In B. S. Dohrenwend, & B. P. Dohrenwend (Eds.), *Stressful life events: Their nature and effects* (pp. 313-331). New York: Wiley & Sons.

Dohrenwned, B. P., & Dohrenwend, B. S. (1969). *Social status and psychological disorder*. New York: Wiley.

Elder, G. H. J. (1985). Perspectives on the life course. In G. H. Elder (Ed.), *Life course dynamics* (pp. 22-49). Ithaca, NY: Cornell University Press.

Elder, G. H. J. (1998). The life course and human development. In R. M. Lerner (Ed.), *Handbook of child psychology, Volume 1: Theoretical models of human development* (pp. 939-991). New York: Wiley.

Ferraro, K. F. (2001). Aging and role transitions. In R. H. Binstock, & L. K. George (Eds.), *Handbook of aging and the social sciences* (5 ed., pp. 313-330). San Diego: Academic Press.

Fiske, A., Gatz, M., & Pedersen, N. L. (2003). Depressive symptoms and aging: The effects of illness and non-health-related events. *Journal of Gerontology: Psychological Sciences, 58B*(6), P320-P328.

Fiske, M., & Chiriboga, D. A. (1990). *Change and continuity in adult life*. San Francisco: Jossey-Bass.

Folkman, S., Lazarus, R. S., Pimley, S., & Novacek, J. (1987). Age differences in stress and coping processes. *Psychology and Aging, 2*(2), 171-184.

George, L. K. (1995). Life events. In G. L. Maddox (Ed.), *The Encyclopedia of Aging* (2 ed., pp. 557-559). New York: Springer.

Glaser, B. G., & Strauss, A. L. (1971). *Status passage: A formal theory*. Mill Valley: Sociology Press.

Goldberg, E. L., & Comstock, G. W. (1980). Epidemiology of life events: Frequency in general populations. *American Journal of Epidemiology, 111*(6), 736-752.

Hägestad, G. O. (1990). Social perspectives on the life course. In R. H. Binstock, & L. K. George (Eds.), *Handbook of aging and social sciences (3ème ed.)*. New York: Academic Press.

Hareven, T. K., & Masaoka, K. (1988). Turning points and transitions: Perceptions of the life course. *Journal of Family History, 13*(3), 271-289.

Heckhausen, J., Dixon, R. A., & Baltes, P. B. (1989). Gains and losses in development throughout adulthood as perceived by different adult age groups. *Developmental Psychology, 25*(1), 109-121.

Johnson, C. L., & Barer, B. M. (1993). Coping and a sense of control among the oldest old: An exploratory analysis. *Journal of Aging Studies, 7*(1), 67-80.

Kane, R. L., Bell, R., Riegler, S., Wilson, A., & Kane, R. A. (1993). Assessing the outcomes of nursing home patients. *Journal of Gerontology, 38*, 385-393.

Katz, S., Downs, T. D., Cash, H. R., & Grotz, R. C. (1970). Progress in development of the index of ADL. *The Gerontologist, 10*(1), 20-30.

Kessler, R. C. (1997). The effects of stressful life events on depression. *Annual Review of Psychology, 48*, 191-214.

Kraaij, V., Arensman, E., & Sopinhoven, P. (2002). Negative life events and depression in elderly persons: A meta-analysis. *Journal of Gerontology: Psychological Sciences, 57B*(1), 87-94.

Lalive d'Epinay, C., Bickel, J.-F., Maystre, C., & Vollenwyder, N. (2000). *Vieillesses au fil du temps. 1979-1994: une révolution tranquille [Old age across the years. 1979-1994: A quiet revolution]*. Lausanne: Réalités sociales.

Mayer, K. U., & Schoepflin, U. (1989). The state and the life course. *Annual Review of Sociology, 15*, 187-209.

McLanahan, S. S., & Sorensen, A. B. (1985). Life events and psychological well-being over the life course. In G. H. Elder (Ed.), *Life course dynamics. Trajectories and transitions, 1968-1980* (pp. 217-238). Ithaca: Cornell University Press.

McLeod, J. D. (1996). Life events. In J. E. Birren (Ed.), *Encyclopedia of gerontology* (Vol. 2, pp. 41-51). San Diego: Academic Press.

McLeod, J. D., & Kessler, R. C. (1990). Socioeconomic status differences in vulnerability to undesirable life events. *Journal of Health and Social Behavior, 31*(2), 162-172.

Pearlin, L. I. (1994). The study of the oldest-old: Some promises and puzzles. *International Journal of Aging and Human Development, 38*(1), 91-98.

Raudenbush, S. W., Bryk, A. S., Cheong, Y. F., & Congdon, R. T., Jr. (2004). *HLM 6: Hierarchical Linear and Nonlinear Modelling* (6 ed.). Lincolnwood, IL: Scientific Software International.

Reese, H. W., & Smyer, M. A. (1983). The dimensionalization of life events. In E. J. Callahan, & K. A. McCluskey (Eds.), *Life-span developmental psychology. Nonnormative life events* (pp. 1-33). New York: Academic Press.

Rosow, I., & Breslau, N. (1966). A Guttman health scale for the aged. *Journal of Gerontology, 21*, 556-559.

Rutter, M. (1996). Transitions and turning points in developmental psychopathology: As applied to the age span between childhood and mid-adulthood. *International Journal of Behavioral Development, 19*(3), 603-626.

Schulenberg, J. E., Maggs, J. L., & O'Malley, P. M. (2003). How and why the understanding of developmental continuity and discontinuity is important. The sample case of long-term consequences of adolescence substance use. In J. T. Mortimer, & M. J. Shanahan (Eds.), *Handbook of the life course* (Vol. 413-436). New York: Kluwer.

Settersten, R. A. (1999). *Lives in time and place. The problems and promises of developmental science*. Amityville: Baywood.

Spini, D., Ghisletta, P., Guilley, E., & Lalive d'Epinay, C. (2007). Frail elderly. In J. E. Birren (Ed.), *Encyclopedia of Gerontology. Age, aging, and the aged* (2nd ed., Vol. 1, pp. 572-579). San Diego: Elsevier, Academic Press.

Stallings, M. C., Dunham, C. C., Gatz, M., Baker, L. A., & Bengtson, V. L. (1997). Relationship among life events and psychological well-being: More evidence for a two-factor theory of well-being. *Journal of Applied Gerontology, 16*(1), 104-119.

Thoits, P. A. (1981). Undesirable life events and psychophysiological distress: A problem of operational confounding. *American Sociological Review, 46*(1), 97-109.

Tudiver, F., Hilditch, J., Permaul, J. A., & McKendree, D. J. (1992). Does mutual help facilitate newly bereaved widowers? . *Evaluation and the Health Professions, 15*, 147-162.

Wang, R. I., Treul, S., & Alverno, L. (1975). A brief self-assessing depression scale. *Journal of Clinical Pharmacology, 15*(2-3), 163-167.

Wheaton, B. (1990). Life transitions, role histories, and mental health. *American Sociological Review, 55*(2), 209-223.

In: The Closing Chapters of Long Lives
Editors: E. Guilley, Ch. J. Lalive d'Epinay

ISBN: 978-1-60456-971-1

Chapter 5

THE DEATH OF A CLOSE RELATIVE OR FRIEND: IMPACT ON HEALTH AND RELATIONSHIPS

Stefano Cavalli**, Luc A. Guillet and Christian J. Lalive d'Epinay

ABSTRACT

The death of a significant other is seen as a major life disruption, with profound consequences for the bereaved person. This type of event occurs more and more frequently with advancing age. In this chapter, the two main questions we endeavor to answer are: in very old age, what are the main sources of bereavement, and what are the consequences of such a loss on health and on relationships?

The bereaved were split according to the category of person being grieved: a close relative or a friend, and then compared with two other groups of non-bereaved elders: one consisting of those who had declared no recent significant change in their life, and the other of those who had reported serious recent health trouble.

This chapter is an upgraded version of a previous paper (Lalive d'Epinay, Cavalli, & Spini, 2003) which was based on the observation of Swilsoo's first octogenarian cohort over a period of five years (1994-1999). Here we used all the data of the completed research, which provided a ten-year follow-up of the first cohort (1994-2004) and a five-year follow-up of the second (1999-2004). Participants on baseline were 652, with a total of 2496 interviews. In the 2003 paper, we used analyses of covariance (ANCOVA); here, we apply multilevel analyses which are especially appropriate for repeated data series.

In very old age, the great majority of the loved ones who die are either siblings or friends. The loss of either a close relative or a friend has an adverse impact on the psychological health of the bereaved, but each person displays a distinctive pattern of consequences. The death of a close relative stimulates a tightening of ties with the family that seems to buffer part of the impact on well-being. No such relational regulation comes into play upon the loss of a friend, with the result that the bereaved person suffers a sharp

---

* The authors wish to thank Dario Spini, co-author of the 2003 paper. Correspondence concerning this chapter should be addressed to Stefano Cavalli, Center for Interdisciplinary Gerontology, Rte de Drize 7, Site Battelle, CH – 1227 Carouge, stefano.cavalli@unige.ch

increase in depressive symptoms; further, the loss of a friend has a delayed disruptive effect on men's sense of closeness.

Death and Its Impact in Later Life

The further a person advances into old age, the more he/she becomes a survivor, i.e. someone whose close relatives and friends have gradually disappeared. Having already snatched the person's ascendants, death now claims the spouse, decimates siblings and friends, and increasingly strikes at later generations. In the circle of family and friends, there are soon as many dead as living. Spousal bereavement is however more typical among the young-old than the old-old. Beyond the age of 80, women greatly outnumber men and most of them are already widows. The men, who are usually married, are still highly likely to die before their spouse. In Switzerland, according to the 2000 census (Swiss Federal Statistical Office, 2000), there are about twice as many women as men in the 80-and-over age bracket. Only 36 per cent of the women still have their spouse, compared with 64 per cent of the men. Advanced old age thus seems to be punctuated by the loss of contemporaries amongst siblings and friends, people with whom the survivor had ties derived from years of sharing rhythms of life, activities, memories and emotions. At the same time, death now seems to strike later generations more frequently than before. According to Moss, Lesher, and Moss (1986), 10% of persons had lost a child when they were over 60, and the risk accentuates with age.

Impact on Health

A good deal has been written about the process of bereavement, the causes of mortality, and the advent and repercussions of widowhood. The literature is scant, however, on the reactions of older people to the death of a child, a sibling or a friend (see Fitzpatrick, 1998).

The excess mortality of the widowed, especially in the year following bereavement, is now well established (Bowling & Windsor, 1995; Carey, 1979-1980; Thierry, 1999, 2000), corroborating the "broken heart" syndrome theory (Parkes, 1972; see also Stroebe & Stroebe, 1993). Spousal bereavement often affects health also: according to Tudiver, Hilditch, Permaul, and McKendree (1992), roughly one person in four incurs problems of physical or psychological health in the first year of widowhood. Nevertheless, as far as the long-term repercussions of widowhood on health are concerned, the findings of research do not all concord. Widowhood does not seem to be associated with worsening physical health (Bennett, 1997; Lalive d'Epinay, Bickel, Maystre, & Vollenwyder, 2000). From the psychosomatic point of view, however, there is agreement that, even after the mourning period, the widowed tend to display more depressive symptoms than their married contemporaries (Delbès & Gaymu, 2000; D. Gallagher, Breckenridge, Thompson, & Peterson, 1983; Lund, Caserta, & Dimond, 1993; Umberson, Wortman, & Kessler, 1992).

The loss of a spouse is undoubtedly a major event but it is not the only instance in which a person with whom one has close affective ties and memories of shared times of life, activities and emotions is taken away. Setting aside the loss of an ascendant, which is an unusual event in old age, let us consider the death of contemporaries (among siblings and friends) and offspring. All in all, the negative consequences of these disappearances appear to be as great as for the loss of a spouse (for the loss of a child, see Arbuckle & de Vries, 1995; Goodman, Rubinstein, Alexander, & Luborsky, 1991; Rogers & Reich, 1988) (for the loss of a brother or sister, see Brubacker, 1985; Moss et al., 1986) (for the loss of a friend, see Fitzpatrick, 1998; Roberto & Stanis, 1994). Some authors have pointed out that, in contrast to the loss of a spouse or close relative, the loss of a friend is not an occasion for any particular recognition or ritual and no specific reaction is organized by those close to the friend in question, which makes coping particularly difficult (Doka, 1989; Sklar & Hartley, 1990). One of the few empirical studies on the subject concluded that those bereft of a friend remained in better health than the control group of non-bereaved (De Vries, Lehman, & Arbuckle, 1995).

Consider for a moment the study by Hays, Gold, and Pieper (1997). Based on a longitudinal survey, the authors compare changes in the health status of four groups of individuals: bereft of a spouse, bereft of a brother or sister, bereft of a friend, and a non-bereaved control group. A comparison of the three bereaved groups shows that it is the loss of a brother or sister that has the greatest impact on the survivors' health. At the same time, the authors detect no significant difference between any of the bereaved groups and the non-bereaved group; all suffered from declining health over the period in question, the decline in functional status and self-rated health even being steeper in the control group than in the bereaved groups! According to the authors, these findings may be accounted for by the heterogeneous composition of the non-bereaved group.

Impact on Relationships

Regarding the impact that the death of a loved one has on relational life, we note some measure of agreement that, with advancing age, the number of social relationships dwindles gradually (see Rook, 2000). But does this mean that relational life wanes? Spousal bereavement, for example, does not necessarily lead to social isolation; on the contrary, the surviving spouse is usually not short of company (Ferraro, Mutran, & Barresi, 1984). Some older people make up for the disappearance of their spouse by strengthening their relationships with friends and their social participation (S. K. Gallagher & Gerstel, 1993). Conversely, other studies conclude that isolation is more acute among widows and widowers (see Wenger, Davies, Shatahmasebi, & Scott, 1996) and that, despite the family's solicitude, the widowed suffer more from loneliness than those who are married (Delbès & Gaymu, 2000; Wenger et al., 1996). Childless couples are particularly exposed to isolation when one of the spouses dies (Johnson & Catalano, 1981).

From a theoretical standpoint, it is important to make a distinction between family and friends. Ties of blood and marriage engender a network in which all the members are related to one another. The death of a close relative is an event for the whole family, prompting a collective ritual and entailing relational adjustments throughout the network. The friendship network, on the other hand, is premised on elective affinities and shared interests that bind an individual to each friend, which in no way prejudges the relations that the friends may have among themselves (Allan, 1979). Based on reciprocal choice, the network of friends consists principally of contemporaries and, in the case of the elderly, of long-time friends; it therefore atrophies drastically in later life, especially as both the opportunities and the desire to make new friends are said to dwindle (S. H. Matthews, 1986). The last-mentioned traits are however disputed (Johnson & Barer, 1997).

Gender

A recent study has shown that the risk of bereavement is greater for older women (65 and over) than for men (Williams, Baker, Allman, & Roseman, 2006). This is a well-known fact as concerns spousal bereavement but, according to the authors, it applies also to the death of other relatives and even friends. Work done in Japan as part of a general population survey confirms this finding and extends its validity to all age brackets, from 10 to 80 (Shimai, 2004). The two studies also concord in finding that the impact of bereavement on the subject's physical and mental health is more pronounced among women than among men.

Other authors are less categorical. Most of the studies on spousal bereavement conclude that widowers encounter more health problems than widows (for exemple Lee, Willets, & Seccombe, 1998; M. A. Matthews, 1991), but there is no unanimity on this point. Lalive d'Epinay et al. (2000) observe no gender difference, while D. Gallagher et al. (1983) note that on the contrary it is women who are more affected mentally.

Various explanations exist for the higher rate of both mortality and morbidity (at least short-term) among men following the spouse's death. According to the paradigm relating to disruptive events and the way they are regulated, the more predictable an event is, the more it can be anticipated and the better it can be tolerated (Lowenthal, Thurner, & Chiriboga, 1975); from this standpoint, spousal bereavement is a possibility that women can accept more easily than men (Lee et al., 1998). Another theory (Aldwin, 1990) focuses on the consequences of a death for the survivor's social network. It is common knowledge that the wife, rather than the husband, is the keeper of the network ; her relational life is richer so she has more people round her when she is deprived of her spouse (Coenen-Huther, Kellerhals, & Von Allmen, 1994; M. A. Matthews, 1991). Moreover, the status of widow, unlike that of widower, is a well-established one recalling the existence of widows' groups always ready to welcome and support 'newcomers'; spousal bereavement thus implies a greater risk of isolation for men. A third approach centers on the reordering of daily life; up to the present at any rate, cohort studies have shown that it is the bereft woman who is better equipped than the man to deal with the tasks of everyday living. These three perspectives (normality and anticipation of the event, network and role, reordering of daily life) together lend weight to the hypothesis that the stress associated with spousal loss is more keenly felt by men (Pearlin, Menaghan, Lieberman, & Mullan, 1981).

Offsetting this, men have the advantage in one respect at least, namely, in their chances of remarrying (Thierry, 1999) or more generally of finding a new soulmate. A qualitative survey carried out successively with a number of widows and widowers aged around 70 showed that nearly all the widowers had found a companion or a friend, without necessarily contemplating marriage or even living together (Groupe "SOL" de l'Université du 3e âge de Genève, 1996).

At this juncture, four comments are called for. First of all, with some quoted exceptions, the empirical studies on the loss of a close relative (other than a spouse) or friend are of a qualitative nature and are based on small samples. Secondly, they deal with the elderly without distinction. According to one hypothesis of the life course theory, however, the likelihood of a given event occurring, and the repercussions of the event, differ depending on the time of life when the event occurs (Elder, 1998). Johnson and Barer (1997) point out, for example, that one characteristic of the very old is their ability to cope with tragic events. Thirdly, most of the studies examine the impact of bereavement a few months or a year after the event. Psychosomatic and relational effects may however come to light much later in the adjustment process. As Fitzpatrick (1998) suggests for morbidity, the analytical plan should be designed to cover both the short and the medium term. Lastly, while the death of a loved one is recognized as being a major disruptive event with repercussions on health and relational life, there is no consensus on the specifics.

Working Hypotheses

Based on a review of the literature, we propose the following hypotheses.

Differential Incidence of Losses of a Loved One

Hypothesis 1: In advanced old age, the source of most bereavements is a sibling or a friend, rather than the spouse or a child.

Impact on Health

Three dimensions of health are distinguished: physical pains, functional health, and psychological health (see next section).

Hypothesis 2: The loss of a close relative or friend adversely affects the health of the surviving elder.

Hypothesis 3: The greatest adverse impact of the loss of a loved one is on the psychological dimension of health.

Impact of Relationships

Two dimensions are distinguished: interactive and affective (see next section).

Hypothesis 4 (family relationships): Considering the systemic nature of the family network and the presence of a bereavement ritual, the loss of a close relative adversely affects the affective dimension, not the interactive dimension.

Hypothesis 5 (relations with friends): Considering the ego-centered organization of the friends network and the lack of a bereavement ritual, the loss of a close friend can be expected to affect adversely both the interactive and the affective dimension.

Gender

We chose here to test the accuracy of the thesis put forward by Williams et al. (2006) on "feminization of bereavement" for older women.

Hypothesis 6: Older women are more liable than men to suffer losses among their loved ones.

Hypothesis 7: The death of a loved one has greater adverse consequences on older women than on men.

With the exception of the first proposition, for which there is ample evidence, these are exploratory hypotheses which will serve as a guide to the analysis of data and interpretation of results.

Finally, previous studies suggest that the time span also has to be taken into account. The effects will therefore be assessed distinguishing the short and longer terms.

METHODS[1]

Respondents

Analyses are based on the data gathered from the 652 community-dwelling elders of both cohorts who were part of Swilsoo at baseline, and with whom 2,496 interviews were carried out.

Measures

Records of Deaths

Spouse, sibling, child. The completed questionnaire provided an exact record of the civil status of the participant and of the number of siblings and children at each wave. At baseline, 69% had at least one sibling, 79% had at least one child. Forty-nine percent of participants were living with their spouse, but here the gender gap was huge: 71% of the men had their spouse at home, but only 27% of the women. From the second wave onwards, the recording of deaths was checked against the information gathered at baseline.

Friend. At baseline, 74% declared that they had a close friend in their network. The recording of deaths of friends started at the second wave of interviews with each cohort, by way of an open question asking whether changes had occurred in the individual's circle of friends since the previous round.

Health

Physical pains. This question listed a number of possible sources of physical suffering (see Lalive d'Epinay et al., 1983 pp. 134-137). Eleven items were proposed: lower limbs, upper limbs, head/face, back, heart, respiratory organs, stomach/abdomen, genital/urinary organs, chest, fever, other. For each item, the respondent reported the degree of his or her suffering on a 3-point scale: no suffering at all, some suffering, suffering a lot. This measure was similar to that used by Kane, Bell, Riegler, Wilson, and Kane (1993) for measuring physical pains, with the difference that they evaluated the frequency of pain. Only the last answer was taken into account across the 11 possible sources of suffering so we in fact used a scale ranging from 0 (no acute suffering) to 11 (11 parts of the body with acute pain). Sample mean at W1 (*SD*) = 0.76 (1.11).

Functional health. The person's ability to perform unaided the essential acts of everyday living (Katz, Downs, Cash, & Grotz, 1970; Lawton & Brody, 1969) was assessed. Included

[1] For a detailed presentation of the Swilsoo research program, see chapter 1.

were five basic activities – washing, dressing and undressing, eating, rising from and going to bed, and moving from one room to another – and three actions involving mobility – moving around outside, walking at least 200 meters, and going up and down stairs. The overall score, ranging from 0 to 16, was the sum of the responses calculated as follows: incapacity (2), some difficulty (1), no difficulty (0). Sample mean at W1 (*SD*) = 1.16 (2.51).

Depressive symptoms (psychological health). Depressive symptoms were recorded by means of the Self-Assessing Depression Scale (SADS, see Wang, Treul, & Alverno, 1975), as adapted by Lalive d'Epinay et al. (1983 pp.127-129). Replies of « never » (0), « rarely » (1), « often » (2) or « always » (3) were recorded for 13 items: feels tired, has trouble sleeping, feels sad, feels lonely, has crying spells or feels like it, feels worried, feels irritable, feels anxious, lacks confidence in the future, lacks appetite, finds time passes slowly, lacks self-confidence, has no pleasure in doing things. This scale ranged from 0 (no symptoms) to 39. Sample mean at W1 (*SD*) = 7.85 (5.58).

Relations with Family and Friends

Two dimensions were distinguished.

The interactive dimension. Based on a record of the frequency (almost never (0), at least once a year (1), once a month (2), once a week (3), almost daily (4)) of visits received, visits made and telephone conversations; range from 0 (no contacts) to 12; sample mean at W1 (*SD*) = 7.05 (2.62) for family relations and 4.93 (2.92) for social relations.

The affective dimension. The indicator used here was the feeling of closeness. The subject was asked how many (a) family members (apart from the spouse), and (b) friends and relatives, he or she has to whom he or she felt "personally very close (loves greatly, feels very concerned about that person's welfare)"; with 3 possible answers 'any', 'one' or 'two or more' for family members and with 4 possible answers 'any', 'one', 'two' or 'three or more' for close friends . (Sample mean at W1 (*SD*) = 1.62 (0.62) for family and 1.68 (1.22) for friends). The absence of anyone who is especially dear is a definition of affective isolation.

Description of Analysis

Two methodological difficulties had to be solved. One concerned the time span over which the impact of bereavement was to be measured and the other related to the definition of the control group or groups.

Time Span

Two temporal measures of the impact of bereavement were introduced: short-term, referring to the interval between two successive waves, and medium-term, referring to the interval between one wave and the next but one. More technically, for the short term, the change on the dependent variable supposedly related to a death occurring between two successive waves (i.e. occurring after W_{n-1} and registered at W_n) was measured at W_n taking into account the value of the dependent variable established at W_{n-1}. For the medium term, the death was recorded in the same way (at W_n) but the change on the dependent variable was measured during the following wave, at W_{n+1} (with reference to the value of the dependent variable at W_{n-1}).

Control Groups: Categorization of the Non-bereaved Elders

If we assume that there is a negative effect on health, for example, a decline among bereaved subjects has to be observed but it is also necessary to demonstrate that the decline is attributable to the bereavement and not to some other event. This was the stumbling-block encountered by Hays et al. (1997) in the above-mentioned study; in comparing the bereaved with the non-bereaved, the authors observed a similar change in health in the two groups. But they did not feel entitled to conclude from this result that the death of a close relative had no specific impact of the survivor's because, they said, of the heterogeneous composition of the control group. Indeed, the latter surely comprised elders who had experienced other kind of losses, most often directly related to their health.

Although Hays et al. did not offer any solution, it can be sought by subdividing the non-bereaved into subgroups and keeping only well homogenized categories. To that end, we took advantage of a question aimed at studying the elders' perception of significant changes in their own life. As from the second wave of our survey, the interview started with the question, "Since our last visit, have there been any important changes in your life?" Affirmative answers were classified according to the life domain on which the change impinged and the valence (positive, negative, and neutral). The classification, with its results, is given in the preceding chapter (see chapter 4).

Table 1 displays the classification based on the self-reported changes (or no changes) among the non-bereaved sequences; 63.8% are the sequences where the elder reported that no important change had occurred in his or her life since the previous interview; 19% reported serious health trouble, and 4.1% a positive change (health improvement, family weddings, birth of an offspring, etc.); the remaining 13.1% were classified as "neutrals" (a change was reported but its valence was unclear) or "others" (the elder reported two or more changes of a different nature or contradictory in valence or in a few cases negative changes not related to health).

Table 1. Bereaved and non-bereaved sequences. Distribution of non-bereaved according to self-reported changes

	n	% on total non-bereaved	% on total sequences
Non-bereaved			
Health trouble changes	284	19.0	15.4
Positive changes	62	4.1	3.3
Neutrals & others	195	13.1	10.6
No change	953	63.8	51.7
Total non-bereaved	1494	100.0	81.0
Total bereaved	350	-	19.0
Total sequences	1844	-	100.0

At that stage, we decided to disregard the categories "other" for its lack of homogeneity, and "positive change" for its relatively small number of sequences (n = 62). We kept the "no change" and the "health trouble change" categories. Comparing the bereaved with the "no change" group provides a measure of the effect attributable to bereavement, while a comparison with the "health trouble" group highlights the differential impact of both kinds of events.

Analyses

Multilevel analyses were applied in comparing the bereaved groups with the "no change" and "health trouble change" groups on the five dependent variables (physical pains, functional health, well-being, interactive dimension and feeling of closeness). Multilevel models were developed for the purpose of analyzing data with multilevel sets (e.g. repeated measures for one individual). They allow the use of repeated measures where both the number of interviews per participant and the time intervals between interviews vary. Furthermore, multilevel analyses can tolerate an incomplete data set because they use all available data instead of restricting the analysis to individuals who participated in all nine waves, thus limiting the selectivity effects (Bryk & Raudenbush, 1992).

A model was tested for each of the five dependent variables. Age (centered on its grand mean), the three categories of change (see below) and the measure of the dependent variables at the previous wave (W_{n-1}) were included as level-1, time-varying predictors; gender as a level-2, time-invariant predictor. Also examined were the possible interaction effects between gender and the three categories. Results were reported with a robust estimation of the standard errors and the effects were tested by the method of restricted maximum likelihood using HLM version 6.0 (Raudenbush, Bryk, Cheong, & Congdon, 2004).

RESULTS

Death Ever-present

Two hundred and thirty-six deaths of close relatives (spouse, siblings and children) and 224 of friends were registered (cf. table 2)[2]. On average, a death was mentioned in one interview out of four. At the end of the first five-year period, more than half of the survivors had lost a close relative, a dear friend, or both. At the end of the ten-year follow-up, seven out of ten survivors (first cohort) had experienced one or more bereavements. Close to half of the losses referred to friends, and four out of ten to siblings, which is by far the most frequent type of loss within the family[3].

---

[2] The difference between the total of 460 bereavements in table 2 and the 350 sequences with recorded bereavements in table 1 is due to the sequences with more than one recorded death.

[3] In the following pages, in three cases out of four the loss of a close relative means the loss of a sibling.

Table 2. Distribution of the deceased by category of decedent

	n	%
Spouse	34	7.4
Child	19	4.1
Sibling	183	39.8
Friend	224	48.7
Total	460	100.0

Table 2 presents the figures for these deaths of relatives and friends, and table 3 a classification according to the gender of the bereaved elders. Although the mean duration of participation in the study was about half a year longer among women, the same proportion of each gender suffered losses, with a higher mean number of deaths reported by men. This last difference results from the fact that men reported more losses of friends than women. Note also that when we take into account only those who have a spouse or siblings, elder women are still more at risk of losing their husband or a sibling.

Bereavement and Health

A comparison with the "no change" group shows that bereavement had a marked short-term impact on well-being (depressive symptoms) and also a distinct impact on functional health (Table 4). The latter impact disappeared with time, while the former waned but remained significant. With regard to the "health trouble" group, it appeared that both kinds of disruptive events had a similar impact on well-being. Of note is the fact that the subjective report of health trouble was corroborated by the measures of physical pains in both the short and the medium term, and on functional health in the short term.

Table 3. Bereaved elders by gender and category of decedent

Gender / Death	Men				Women				Total			
	n	M	%[1]	%[2]	n	M	%[1]	%[2]	n	M	%[1]	%[2]
Spouse	18	1.0	5.5	7.7	16	1.0	5.0	18.4	34	1.0	5.2	10.6
Child	12	1.1	3.7	4.5	6	1.0	1.9	2.4	18	1.0	2.8	3.5
Sibling	51	1.5	15.5	22.7	73	1.5	22.6	32.6	124	1.5	19.0	27.6
Friend	59	2.5	17.9	-	42	1.9	13.0	-	101	2.2	15.5	-
Total bereaved elders	111	2.3	33.7	-	112	1.9	34.7	-	223	2.2	34.2	-
Participants at baseline	329				323				652			
Mean duration of participation (years)	5.5				5.9				5.7			

[1] % of total participants.

[2] % of total of those who had such a relative (or close friend) at baseline.

Bereavement and Relations with Family and Friends

Turning to the repercussions that the loss of someone close may have on the relationships of the elderly, we took two aspects into consideration: the interactive dimension (contacts) and the affective dimension (the feeling of closeness). From the outset, we subdivided the bereaved according to the category of decedent involved and, logically, we analyzed the impact of the loss of a close relative on *family life* (Table 5) and that of a friend on *social, extra familial life* (Table 6). In tables 5 and 6, the three measures of health are included, in order to check whether the two categories of bereavement have the same kind of impact or not.

When compared with the "no change" group, *losses in the family* had two kinds of effect: in the short term, there was a strengthening of contacts with the family but on the other hand there was a negative impact on well-being and on functional health (Table 5). The intensification of family interaction was also evident when the bereaved persons were compared with the "health trouble" group. But neither of these effects lasted in the medium term.

Unlike the loss of a close relative, *the death of a friend* was not followed by a surge in social exchanges (Table 6). In the short term the grief was associated with a sharp increase in depressive symptoms, while in the medium term there was a weakening of the sense of closeness. Here a gender effect was registered, the last-mentioned trend being specific to men!

Table 4. Death of a loved one: relation to health (physical pains, functional impairments and depressive symptoms). Bereaved group compared with "health trouble" and "no change" groups (multilevel analysis)

Bereaved	versus No change		versus Health trouble change	
n of sequences	953		284	
Dep. variables	Coeff.	P.value	Coeff.	P.value
Short term				
Physical pains	0.08	0.293	-0.26	0.009**
Functional impairments	0.29	0.044*	-0.92	<0.001***
Depressive symptoms	1.15	<0.001***	0.14	0.672
Medium term				
Physical pains	-0.01	0.967	-0.34	0.005**
Functional impairments	0.02	0.918	-0.58	0.061
Depressive symptoms	0.76	0.021*	-0.02	0.962

Note: Age and sex are controlled. Bereaved: n = 350. * $p \leq .05$. ** $p \leq .01$. *** $p \leq .001$. Physical pains: scale ranging from 0 (no acute suffering) to 11 (11 parts of the body with acute pain). Functional health: scale ranging from 0 (no disability or difficulty) to 16 (8 disabilities). Depressive symptoms: scale ranging from 0 (no depressive symptoms) to 39.

Table 5. Death of a close relative: relation to health and family life. Family bereaved compared to "health trouble" and "no change" groups (multilevel analysis)

Family bereaved	versus No change		versus Health trouble change	
n of sequences	953		284	
Dep.variables	Coeff.	P.value	Coeff.	P.value
Short term				
Health				
Physical pains	0.07	0.519	-0.30	0.017*
Functional impairments	0.33	0.047*	-0.97	0.001***
Depressive symptoms	0.83	0.016*	-0.24	0.552
Family life				
Interactive dimension	0.37	0.026*	0.47	0.033*
Feeling of closeness	0.05	0.103	0.06	0.067
Medium term				
Health				
Physical pains	0.08	0.531	-0.39	0.006**
Functional impairments	0.15	0.490	-0.80	0.018*
Depressive symptoms	0.70	0.054	-0.30	0.525
Family life				
Interactive dimension	0.19	0.259	0.31	0.217
Feeling of closeness	0.02	0.580	0.06	0.218

Note: Age and sex are controlled. Bereaved: n = 350. * $p \leq .05$. ** $p \leq .01$. *** $p \leq .001$. Physical pains: scale ranging from 0 (no acute suffering) to 11 (11 parts of the body with acute pain). Functional impairments: scale ranging from 0 (no disability or difficulty) to 16 (8 disabilities). Depressive symptoms: scale ranging from 0 (no depressive symptoms) to 39. Interactive dimension: scale ranging from 0 (no contact) to 12. Feeling of closeness: scale ranging from 0 (no very close person) to 2 or more.

The Hypotheses Revisited

Sources of bereavement (Hyp. 1): Our results confirmed that in very old age, the two main sources of bereavement are siblings and friends. The fact that as many as three out of four deaths among close relatives (children, spouses, siblings) are siblings may be a surprise.

Health (Hyp. 2-3): We postulated that there is an overall effect on health, but that the psychological impact is greater than the impact on physical or functional dimensions. The only attested relationship with the latter is between the loss of a close relative and functional health (Hyp. 2). Psychologically, bereavement is clearly associated with an increase in depressive symptoms. This impact on well-being is more acute in the case of the loss of a friend than in that of loss of a close relative, but it is manifest in both cases (Hyp. 3).

Table 6. Death of a friend: relation to health and social life. Loss of friend compared to "health trouble" and "no change" groups (multilevel analysis)

Loss of friend	versus No change		versus Health trouble change	
n of sequences	953		284	
Dep.variables	Coeff.	P.value	Coeff.	P.value
Short term				
Health				
Physical pains	0.13	0.266	-0.24	0.065
Functional impairments	0.18	0.209	-1.10	<0.001***
Depressive symptoms	1.25	<0.001***	0.04	0.916
Social life				
Interactive dimension	-0.24	0.285	-0.02	0.930
Feeling of closeness	-0.01	0.988	0.03	0.663
Medium term				
Health				
Physical pains	0.13	0.285	-0.30	0.030*
Functional impairments	-0.30	. 0.068	-1.09	<0.001***
Depressive symptoms	0.61	0.185	-0.26	0.652
Social life				
Interactive dimension	0.41	0.090	0.26	0.411
Feeling of closeness	-0.32	0.015*[1]	-0.19	0.189

Note: Age and sex are controlled. Bereaved: n = 350. * $p \leq .05$. ** $p \leq .01$. *** $p \leq .001$. Physical pains: scale ranging from 0 (no acute suffering) to 11 (11 parts of the body with acute pain). Functional impairments: scale ranging from 0 (no disability or difficulty) to 16 (8 disabilities). Depressive symptoms: scale ranging from 0 (no depressive symptoms) to 39. Interactive dimension: scale ranging from 0 (no contact) to 12. Feeling of closeness: scale ranging from 0 (no very close person) to 3 or more.

[1] Interaction with gender: coeff. = -0.34 (p-value = 0.043*). When a bereavement occurred, the feeling of closeness of women, contrary to men, did not decrease.

Family and extrafamilial life (Hyp. 4-5): The idea of contrasting the systemic nature of the family network with the ego-centered nature of the friends' network was valid, but it has to be amended in the light of the results: the family reacts to the death of one of its members by intensifying exchanges in the short term, offering support to the mourning elder. With the passage of time, however, the tempo of exchanges returns to normal (Hyp. 4). As expected, no similar reaction from the friends' network was observed. But we hypothesized that the loss would adversely affect both the interactive and the affective dimension. The former was confirmed but not the latter: in the medium term the feeling of having a close friend (sense of closeness) was fading (but only among the men; see below) (Hyp. 5).

Gender (Hyp. 6-7): It was confirmed that in very old age losing a spouse is no longer a frequent event, but also that the few remaining married women were still more likely than married men to become widowed. As for the risk of losing a loved one, it seemed to impinge equally on both women and men, although differences were observed according to the category of decedent, with women more often bereft of siblings, and men more often of friends (Hyp.6).

Gender was introduced as control variable in every multilevel analysis. The only significant interaction related to the medium-term impact of the loss of a friend on the affective dimension: this was specific to men. With this exception, all the negative consequences of bereavement were equally shared by both genders (Hyp.7). Our data do not substantiate the "feminization of bereavement" thesis.

DISCUSSION AND CONCLUSION

Bearing in mind the reservations of Hay et al. (1997) concerning the inadequacy of their non-bereaved group as control because of its heterogeneity (deriving from the various sources of possible events that impinged on the elders' life), we decided to split the non-bereaved into homogeneous groups, separating those reporting no important change in their life recently from those who declared a recent serious health problem.

Thanks to this analytical design, the distinctive implications of two kinds of bereavement (bereft of a close relative, of a friend) on health and social life could be traced, and also compared with those due to health trouble. Firstly, while the elders reporting health trouble suffer a decline in their physical and functional health and also an increase in depressive symptoms, bereavement mainly strikes at psychological health. Secondly, the pattern of impact varies depending on the tie between the elder and the deceased. The death of a close relative impacts the functional dimension of health, which is not the case with the loss of a friend. Thirdly, the death of a close relative stimulates exchanges within the family network in the short term, and this phenomenon seems to have a protective effect on psychological health: an increase in depressive symptoms is noted but it is distinctly less pronounced than that observed after the loss of a friend. Further, the loss of a close relative has no repercussions on the feeling of closeness within the family, and this may be due to the fact that the family network offers alternatives to the elders' affective needs. When a close friend dies, no regulation appears to be put into motion by the network. One short-term effect is a steep increase in depressive symptoms; in the medium term, the elders become aware that they have lost one of the few – maybe their only – surviving close friends. Our findings concord with the fact that, in contrast to the loss of a relative, that of a friend is not an occasion for any specific ritual or action of the part of those close; thus the bereaved remains alone with his/her grief (Doka, 1989; Sklar & Hartley, 1990). More generally, our results show that bereavement is a good tracer of the differences in structure and in functioning of each network, the systemic nature of the family network with its resilience, the ego-centred one of the friends' network with its rigidity.

In the short term, mourning a close relative or a friend has a noticeable impact on the (mainly psychological) health and on the relational life of the elders, but as time goes by, this very disruptive event seems to be regulated in the medium term and the situation returns to normal. Here, normal means: not different from the situation displayed by their "no change" contemporaries, but with two exceptions: first, elders mourning their spouse or a child seem to suffer from a lasting decline in their morale; and second, men bereft of friends have a weakening sense of closeness, the exception here being that, at that age, especially for men, it is difficult to find a substitute for the loss of a close friend and the feeling of being a survivor intensifies.

By and large, however, after the period of mourning, the regulation is over and done with. Going against the mainstream of research on bereavement, which focuses on its disruptive effects, especially on health, Dutton and Zisoock (2005) underline people's ability to cope with it: "Accumulating evidence suggests that resilience to grief in face of bereavement is the norm, rather than an exception". This study does not relate to old age in particular, but the resilience of persons in coping with the various misfortunes that afflict old age has been noted, for example, by Johnson and Barer (1997); Pearlin (1994), and others. Our study brings fresh evidence of the considerable impact that bereavement of a loved one has on the psychological health of the elders, and of the elders' potential of resilience.

As far as gender is concerned, we could not find evidence of any "feminization of bereavement" in advanced old age. Obviously, one of the various consequences of the increasing feminization of the population with advancing old age is that women, having a longer life, will have to cope with more bereavements and will more frequently be put in the position of a survivor than men. But for those elders who share the same very old age, the Grim Reaper seems to treat the two genders in a very even-handed – and tough – way. The only differential impact related to gender is, in the medium term, the decrease in the feeling of closeness among the old men, a result that bears out not only Matthews' observation that women are the social network keepers (S. H. Matthews, 1986) but also the claim by Johnson and Barer that women are more skilled at making new friends (Johnson & Barer, 1997).

The methodological strength of our research was that we were able to disentangle the "non-bereaved" groups, which allowed us to trace the consequences of bereavement and to bring to light the distinctive patterns of consequences when the bereaved mourns a close relative or friend. Compared with our 2003 paper, which was based on the first five-year follow-up of a single cohort, the current analyses, carried out with the completed data on two cohorts (with twice as many elders and two-and-a-half times more interviews), revealed some effects not visible then (e.g. the short-term impact of the death of a relative on functional health, the medium-term degradation of the feeling of closeness when a friend is mourned), results which led to a better understanding of the two grieving processes.

The Swilsoo program centers on the life trajectories of the oldest old, who now constitute the fastest growing age group in Western countries and at the same time the group suffering from the greatest dearth of social research. The possibilities for comparison of the Swilsoo data with other studies are thus rare. Another limitation is that our study focused on the morbidity, not the mortality, ensuing from bereavement. One of our conclusions was that the oldest old have proved to be very resilient to bereavement; it would be more accurate to say that the survivors have proved to be so. Suggestions for future work are as follows:

(a) A more complete picture could be obtained by widening the list of family decedent categories (to include at least in-laws and grandchildren); a comparative analysis of the impact of bereavement by type of kinship tie with the deceased person would be worthwhile but would require large samples;
(b) The flexibility of the family system stems mainly from its multigenerational nature. This being so, what is the situation when the older person loses a brother or sister and has no offspring (20% of our elders belonged to a one-generation family)?

(c) Generalizations and age-specific conclusions could be arrived at by extending the samples to other periods of the life course.

REFERENCES

Aldwin, C. (1990). The Elders Life Stress Inventory (ELSI): Egocentric and nonegocentric stress. In M. A. P. Stephens, S. E. Hobfoll, J. H. Crowther, & D. L. Tennenbaum (Eds.), *Stress and coping in late life families* (pp. 49-69). New York: Hemisphere.

Allan, G. (1979). *A sociology of friendship and kinship*. London: George Allen & Unwin.

Arbuckle, N. W., & de Vries, B. (1995). The long-term effects of later life spousal and parental bereavement on personal functioning. *The Gerontologist, 35*, 637-647.

Bennett, K. M. (1997). Widowhood in elderly women: The medium- and long-term effects on mental and physical health. *Mortality, 2*(137-148).

Bowling, A., & Windsor, J. (1995). Death after widow(er)hood: An analysis of mortality rates up to 13 years after bereavement. *Omega: Journal of Death and Dying, 31*(35-49).

Brubacker, T. (1985). *Later life families*. Beverly Hills: Sage.

Bryk, A. S., & Raudenbush, S. W. (1992). *Hierarchical Linear Models; Applications and data analysis methods*. Newbury Park, CA: Sage Publications.

Carey, R. G. (1979-1980). Weathering widowhood: Problems and adjustment of the widowed during the first year. *Omega: Journal of Death and Dying, 10*(2), 163-174.

Coenen-Huther, J., Kellerhals, J., & Von Allmen, M. (1994). *Les réseaux de solidarité dans la famille*. Lausanne: Réalités Sociales.

De Vries, B., Lehman, A. J., & Arbuckle, N. W. (1995, November). *Reactions to the death of a close friend in later life.* Paper presented at the annual meeting of the Gerontological Society of America, Los Angeles.

Delbès, C., & Gaymu, J. (2000). Du veuvage à l'isolement. *Gérontologie et Société*(95), 11-26.

Doka, K. J. (1989). *Disenfranchised grief: Recognizing hidden sorrow.* New York: Lexington Books.

Dutton, Y., & Zisook, S. (2005). Adaptation to bereavement. *Death Studies, 29*(10), 877-903.

Elder, G. H. J. (1998). The life course and human development. In R. M. Lerner (Ed.), *Handbook of child psychology, Volume 1: Theoretical models of human development* (pp. 939-991). New York: Wiley.

Ferraro, K. F., Mutran, E., & Barresi, C. M. (1984). Widowhood, health, and friendship support in later life. *Journal of Health and Social Behavior, 25*, 245-259.

Fitzpatrick, T. R. (1998). Bereavement events among elderly men: The effects of stress and health. *Journal of Applied Gerontology, 17*(2), 204-228.

Gallagher, D., Breckenridge, J., Thompson, L. W., & Peterson, J. A. (1983). Effects of bereavement on indicators of mental health in elderly widows and widowers. *Journal of Gerontology, 38*, 565-571.

Gallagher, S. K., & Gerstel, N. (1993). Kinkeeping and friend keeping among older women: The effect of marriage. *The Gerontologist, 33*, 675-681.

Goodman, M., Rubinstein, R. L., Alexander, B. B., & Luborsky, M. (1991). Cultural differences among elderly women in coping with the death of an adult child. *Journal of Gerontology, 46*, 321-329.

Groupe "SOL" de l'Université du 3e âge de Genève. (1996). *Vivre sans elle. Le veuvage au masculin*. Genève: Georg.

Hays, J. C., Gold, D. T., & Pieper, C. F. (1997). Sibling bereavement in late life. *Omega: Journal of Death and Dying, 35*(1), 25-42.

Johnson, C. L., & Barer, B. M. (1997). *Life beyond 85 years. The aura of survivorship*. New York: Springer.

Johnson, C. L., & Catalano, D. J. (1981). Childless elderly and their family support. *The Gerontologist*, 610-618.

Kane, R. L., Bell, R., Riegler, S., Wilson, A., & Kane, R. A. (1993). Assessing the outcomes of nursing home patients. *Journal of Gerontology, 38*, 385-393.

Katz, S., Downs, T. D., Cash, H. R., & Grotz, R. C. (1970). Progress in development of the index of ADL. *The Gerontologist, 10*(1), 20-30.

Lalive d'Epinay, C., Bickel, J.-F., Maystre, C., & Vollenwyder, N. (2000). *Vieillesses au fil du temps. 1979-1994: une révolution tranquille [Old age across the years. 1979-1994: a quiet revolution]*. Lausanne: Réalités sociales.

Lalive d'Epinay, C., Cavalli, S., & Spini, D. (2003). The death of a loved one: Impact on health and relationships in very old age. *Omega: Journal of Death and Dying, 47*(3), 265-284.

Lalive d'Epinay, C., Cavalli, S., & Vascotto Karkin, B. (2000). *Events that change one's life in the course of very old age* Poster session presented at the annual meeting of the Gerontological Society of America, Washington DC.

Lalive d'Epinay, C., Christe, E., Coenen-Huther, J., Hagmann, H.-M., Jeanneret, O., Junod, J.-P., et al. (1983). *Vieillesses: situations, itinéraires et modes de vie des personnes âgées aujourd'hui [Old ages: Life conditions, life trajectories and life styles]*. Saint-Saphorin: Georgi.

Lawton, M. P., & Brody, E. M. (1969). Assessment of older people: Self-maintaining and instrumental activities of daily living. *The Gerontologist, 9*, 179-186.

Lee, G. R., Willets, M. C., & Seccombe, K. (1998). Widowhood and depression: Gender differences. *Research on Aging, 20*, 611-630.

Lowenthal, M. F., Thurner, M., & Chiriboga, D. A. (1975). *Four stages of life*. San Francisco: Jossey-Bass.

Lund, D. A., Caserta, M. S., & Dimond, M. F. (1993). The course of spousal bereavement in later life. In M. S. Stroebe, W. Stroebe, & R. O. Hansson (Eds.), *Handbook of bereavement* (pp. 240-254). New York: Cambridge University Press.

Matthews, M. A. (1991). *Widowhood in Later Life*. Toronto et Vancouver: Butterworths.

Matthews, S. H. (1986). Friendship in old age: Biography and circumstances. In V. W. Marshall (Ed.), *Later life: The social psychology of aging* (pp. 233-266). Beverly Hills: Sage.

Moss, M. S., Lesher, E. L., & Moss, S. Z. (1986). Impact of the death of an adult child on elderly parents: Some observations. *Omega: Journal of Death and Dying, 17*(3), 209-218.

Parkes, C. M. (1972). *Bereavement: Studies of grief in the adult life*. New York: International Universities Press.

Pearlin, L. I. (1994). The study of the oldest-old: some promises and puzzles. *International Journal of Aging and Human Development, 38*(1), 91-98.

Pearlin, L. I., Menaghan, E. G., Lieberman, M. A., & Mullan, J. T. (1981). The stress process. *Journal of Health and Social Behavior, 22*, 337-356.

Raudenbush, S. W., Bryk, A. S., Cheong, Y. F., & Congdon, R. T., Jr. (2004). *HLM 6: Hierarchical Linear and Nonlinear Modelling* (6 ed.). Lincolnwood, IL: Scientific Software International.

Roberto, K. A., & Stanis, P. I. (1994). Reactions of older women to the death of their close friends. *Omega: Journal of Death and Dying, 29*(1), 17-27.

Rogers, M. P., & Reich, P. (1988). On the health consequences of bereavement. *New England Journal of Medicine, 319*, 510-512.

Rook, K. S. (2000). The evolution of social relationships in later adulthood. In S. H. Qualls, & N. Abeles (Eds.), *Psychology and the aging revolution. How we adapt to longer life* (pp. 173-191). Washington DC: American Psychology Association.

Shimai, S. (2004). Bereavement experience in the general population: Incidence, consequences, and coping in a national sample of Japan. *Omega: Journal of Death and Dying, 48*(2), 137-147.

Sklar, F., & Hartley, S. F. (1990). Close friends as survivors: Bereavement patterns in a hidden population. *Omega: Journal of Death and Dying, 21*(103-112).

Stroebe, M. S., & Stroebe, W. (1993). The mortality of bereavement: A review. In M. S. Stroebe, W. Stroebe, & R. O. Hansson (Eds.), *Handbook of bereavement* (pp. 175-195). New York: Cambridge University Press.

Swiss Federal Statistical Office. (2000). The 2000 population census. 2008, from http://www.bfs.admin.ch/bfs/portal/fr/index.html

Thierry, X. (1999). Risques de mortalité et de surmortalité au cours des dix premières années de veuvage. *Population, 54*(2), 177-204.

Thierry, X. (2000). Mortel veuvage. Risques de mortalité et causes médicales des décès aux divers moments du veuvage. *Gérontologie et Société, 95*, 27-45.

Tudiver, F., Hilditch, J., Permaul, J. A., & McKendree, D. J. (1992). Does mutual help facilitate newly bereaved widowers? *Evaluation and the Health Professions, 15*, 147-162.

Umberson, D., Wortman, C. B., & Kessler, R. C. (1992). Widowhood and depression: Explaining long-term gender differences in vulnerability. *Journal of Health and Social Behavior*(33), 10-24.

Wang, R. I., Treul, S., & Alverno, L. (1975). A brief self-assessing depression scale. *Journal of Clinical Pharmacology, 15*(2-3), 163-167.

Wenger, G. C., Davies, R., Shatahmasebi, S., & Scott, A. (1996). Social isolation and loneliness in old age: Review and model refinement. *Ageing and Society, 16*(3), 333-358.

Williams, B. R., Baker, P. S., Allman, R. M., & Roseman, J. M. (2006). The feminization of bereavement among community-dwelling older adults. *Journal of Women and Aging, 18*(3), 3-18.

PART 3: SOCIAL NETWORKS AND RELATIONSHIPS OF THE ELDERS

In: The Closing Chapters of Long Lives
Editors: E. Guilley, Ch. J. Lalive d'Epinay

ISBN: 978-1-60456-971-1

Chapter 6

GIVING AND RECEIVING INSTRUMENTAL SUPPORT WITHIN THE FAMILY NETWORK

Franca Armi*[*], *Edith Guilley and Christian J. Lalive d'Epinay

ABSTRACT

Research on social support typically focuses only on support that the elderly receive from their social networks. The aim of this chapter is to analyze the exchange of services between the very old and their family. We hypothesize that elders with declining health will try to maintain the provision of services, even when they require and receive help. We address the issue of support exchanges in a random sample of two cohorts of community-dwelling octogenarians participating in the Swiss Interdisciplinary Longitudinal Study on the Oldest Old (Swilsoo). We use a multilevel model to assess the effect of health (operationalized in three statuses: ADL-dependent, ADL-independent frail, and robust) on the frequency of services that the old persons provide and receive from their family. Our results show that the recourse by very old persons to instrumental support from their family is linked to their health status. Being ADL-dependent drastically alters the capacity to provide services. Elders affected by frailty maintain the support they provide to their family at the same level as robust elders do. This highlights the importance in old age of preserving a positive and active role within the family.

INTRODUCTION

Throughout adult life, individuals try to reciprocate the support they receive (Wentowsky, 1981). Reciprocity in giving and receiving help has been found to be associated with life satisfaction and self-esteem (Liang, Krause, & Bennett, 2001) and providing services to others endows individuals with a positive role (Boerner & Reinhardt, 2003; Krause,

[*] Correspondence concerning this chapter should be addressed to Franca Armi, Center for Interdisciplinary Gerontology, Rte de Drize 7, Site Battelle, CH – 1227 Carouge, armif@bluewin.ch

Herzog, & Baker, 1992). Conversely, when 'giving' is difficult or even impossible and only 'taking' occurs, people feel uncomfortable with the imbalance (Liang et al., 2001). Health problems are one reason for a person to limit his/her support to others because certain services then become difficult to carry out. This applies particularly to very old age, when health problems may endanger reciprocity in giving and receiving help. However, the situation regarding the exchange of services between the very old and their family is little known. Research has widely considered the very old as support recipients and far less as support providers. Some studies have dealt with caregiver activity in advanced old age but they focus mainly on the disabled or dependent people (Becker, Beyene, Newsom, & Mayen, 2003; Boerner & Reinhardt, 2003). More representative studies are therefore needed. In particular, additional research should investigate the service exchanges of frail persons, who constitute the majority in very old age (Guilley et al., 2008). In this chapter, we take into consideration all of the oldest old, the dependent as well as the robust and the frail.

Since providing services to others bestows a positive role on people, especially older people, our hypothesis is that elders will try to maintain this role as long as possible even when frailty affects their daily life. Our main objectives in this chapter are: (a) to gauge whether the amount of instrumental support received by very old persons from their family is linked to their health status, (b) to assess the extent to which frail persons and ADL-dependent persons still help their family, and (c) to identify the socio-demographic factors that influence the support provided and received in advanced old age.

METHODS

Participants

For this chapter we used data obtained from the two cohorts of the Swiss Interdisciplinary Longitudinal Study on the Oldest Old (Swilsoo). We focused on 691 community-dwelling participants, which represented a total of 2,623 interviews across the study (please see chapter 1 for a description of the sample). The mean age at baseline was 81.8 (+/-1.4) years.

Measures

Our attention centered on services exchanged with non-household family members, with the emphasis on instrumental supports. Two series of questions assessed the frequency with which instrumental aids were provided[1] by the very old person or received[2] from non-household family members. A choice of four possible answers was offered: "never", "rarely", "every month", and "at least once a week". With regard to the question on services provided

[1] Seven services were taken into account: (1) performing household tasks, bringing or preparing meals; (2) doing the shopping; (3) doing repairs and odd jobs, gardening; (4) making clothes or other items; (5) taking a member of the family for a walk or to a show, a café or a restaurant; (6) helping a member of the family in his or her occupational activities; (7) looking after the children, seeing that they do their homework.

[2] Six services were taken into account: (1) performing household tasks; (2) bringing or preparing meals; (3) doing the shopping; (4) doing repairs and odd jobs, gardening; (5) helping to complete income tax returns and insurance claims; (6) helping with toilet activities (taking a bath, doing hair).

by the participants (n=2,410 interviews) proxy respondents were excluded at each wave, whereas they were excluded at baseline for services received from non-household family members (n=2,623 interviews). The proxy respondents were more likely to be older and in worse functional health than the self-respondents, who otherwise were similar in terms of gender. Those questions enabled us to construct frequency scores by averaging out the different answers given.

Health is operationalized in three statuses: ADL-dependent, ADL-independent frail, and robust. A participant was considered ADL-dependent if he/she was unable to perform alone at least one of five activities of daily living (washing, dressing and undressing, eating, rising from and going to bed, and moving around the living quarters (cf. Katz, Ford, Moskowitz, Jackson, & Jaffee, 1963). Participants without incapacities on ADL but suffering from two or more deficiencies in five health domains (sensoriality, mobility, memory, energy and physical ailments) were considered as ADL-independent frail, and participants without ADL incapacities and having less that two deficiencies in the above-mentioned health domains were considered as robust (for further details, see Guilley et al., 2008).

The family network was assessed by standard questions about household composition (living alone or not) and the existence of living siblings and descendants (children, grandchildren or great grandchildren).

The socio-demographic variables used in the study included birth cohort, age, gender, geographical area (urban or semi-rural area) and socio-economic status (working-class or middle/upper-class). Socio-economic status was assessed as a composite of education, income and socio-occupational categories.

Plan of Analysis

The objective was to investigate the effects of participants' health status on the frequency of (1) services provided by the very old participants and (2) services received from their family network, controlling for socio-demographic variables and family network variables, using multilevel analyses. Multilevel analyses can tolerate an incomplete data set because they use all available data instead of restricting the analysis to survivals (Bryk & Raudenbush, 1992) and therefore limit the selectivity effects.

The two above-mentioned models used several waves of assessment (up to nine for the first cohort, up to five for the second one). Age (centered on its grand mean), health status, household composition and the presence of descendants were included as level-1, time-varying predictors; and birth cohort, gender, socio-economic status, and geographical area as level-2, time-invariant predictors. The 'geographical area' variable was considered to be time-invariant because participants who moved away from the two sampled areas were excluded from the survey.

The construction of the models was divided into three steps. First, we included birth cohort, socio-demographic variables and health status (with ADL-independent frail as the reference). Second, we added separately the family network variables and interactions between socio-demographic variables, as well as interactions between socio-demographic variables and health status. Third, the variables or interactions found to be significantly related to frequency of support in the second step were considered in subsequent multivariate modeling. Results were reported with a robust estimation of the standard errors and the effects were tested by the method of restricted maximum likelihood using HLM version 6 (Raudenbush, Bryk, Cheong, & Congdon, 2004).

RESULTS

Although 43.0% of the participants were living alone at baseline, many of the very old still possessed a family network: 79.1% of the participants had at least one living descendant (child, grandchild or great grandchild) and 69.1% still had at least one living brother or sister (Table 1). The proportion of robust individuals at baseline was 43.4%, ADL-independent frail individuals 49.5%, and ADL-dependent subjects only 7.1%. The ADL-independent frail category was thus the leading health status among the study participants and may be seen as a "buffer" category between robustness and ADL-dependence. At baseline 31.9% of the persons, notwithstanding their advanced age, were providing at least one service to their non-household family members and 33.3% were receiving at least one service from their family.

The frequency of services that the participants received from their family networks was a function of their health status: robust individuals received less frequent support and ADL-dependent individuals more frequent support compared to ADL-independent frail subjects (Table 2).

The provision of services by the very old person was also altered by his/her health, but in a non-linear form. The group of ADL-dependent persons stood apart from the other two groups in that they offered distinctly fewer aids. In contrast, the frequency of aid offered to the family was the same for both ADL-independent frail and robust persons.

Table 1. Characteristics at baseline and their evolution across the study (N=691)

Domain	Characteristics	At baseline N (%)[1]
Socio-demographic	Gender (woman)	345 (49.9)
	Socio-economic status (middle/upper-class)	325 (47.0)
	Geographical area (urban)	353 (51.1)
Health status	Robust	297 (43.4)
	ADL-independent frail	341 (49.5)
	ADL-dependent	49 (7.1)
Family networks	Lives alone	297 (43.0)
	Has at least one descendant	546 (79.1)
	Has at least one sibling	475 (69.1)
Exchanges of services with family (every month)[2]	Provides at least one service	202 (31.9)
	Receives at least one service	212 (33.3)

[1] Percentages are given for subjects without missing values.
[2] Household members excluded.

The health status of the elderly was not the only factor determining the frequency of exchanges of services with their family. While the support provided by very old people diminished in the course of the study period, the services received by octogenarians from their family increased. As could be expected, having one or more descendants substantially increased the frequency of the services which the persons both provided and received. Persons without a cohabitant – who, when present, was the principal caregiver – received more services from the rest of the family but provided services to their family with the same frequency as persons living with a cohabitant. The region of residence was also a factor determining the frequency of exchanges of services, the persons living in the urban area receiving and providing fewer services. This effect was more marked for individuals of the first Swilsoo cohort. Lastly, persons of middle or upper socio-economic status received fewer services from their family; this effect being more pronounced for the robust participants.

DISCUSSION

This study was motivated by three questions: (a) Is the amount of instrumental support received by very old persons from their family linked to their health status?; (b) To what extent do frail and ADL-dependent persons still help their family?; (c) What other socio-demographic factors influence the support provided and received in advanced old age?

Table 2. Effects (regression coefficient (standard error)) of potential determinants on the average frequency of services exchanged between the very old persons and their family network

Domain	Characteristics	Services provided (N=2,410 interviews)	Services received (N=2,623 interviews)
Socio-demographic	Birth cohort (1915-1919 *vs* 1910-1914)	-0.11 (0.03)***	-0.20 (0.05)***
	Age (years)	-0.02 (0.00)***	0.02 (0.01)*
	Gender (woman)	-0.00 (0.02)	0.05 (0.03)
	Socio-economic status (middle/upper-class)	0.02 (0.02)	-0.22 (0.06)***
	Geographic area (urban)	-0.08 (0.03)**	-0.26 (0.06)***
Health status	Robust *vs* ADL-independent frail	0.02 (0.01)	-0.13 (0.03)***
	ADL-dependent *vs* ADL-independent frail	-0.06 (0.02)**	0.20 (0.04)***
Family networks	Lives alone	/	0.18 (0.03)***
	Has at least one descendant	0.08 (0.02)***	0.26 (0.02)***
Interactions	Cohort x geographical area	0.10 (0.03)**	0.16 (0.05)**
	Cohort x socio-economic status	/	0.07 (0.05)
	Age x socio-economic status	/	-0.01 (0.01)
	Robust x socio-economic status	/	0.10 (0.03)**
	Robust x geographical area	/	0.04 (0.03)
	Socio-economic status x geographical area	/	0.10 (0.05)

*: $p<0.05$; **: $p<0.01$; ***: $p<0.001$; / : variables not included in multivariate modeling because of their insignificant effects in univariate modeling.

Each category of persons – robust, ADL-independent frail and ADL-dependent – received a different level of aid from their family, and we have shown here that aid goes to those who need it most. Recourse to the family network increased in parallel with the process of frailty. Similar results were found for the recourse to formal help (Armi, Guilley, & Lalive d'Epinay, in press)

Another finding of this study relates to a subject rarely dealt with in the literature, namely, the caregiver activity of very old people. At baseline, 31.9% of the participants provided services to their non-household family members. This challenges the assumption that informal caregivers are overwhelmingly middle-aged people. The level of this support was however seriously reduced in the case of ADL-dependent persons. This is in line with other results obtained by van Tilburg and Broese van Groenou (2002), who demonstrated that decline in functional ability predicted a drastic decrease in the provision of instrumental support. Studies in the field of intergenerational exchanges show that old persons do not necessarily see this diminished capacity to give services as a debt, on the grounds that the services they currently receive may make up for the many services they have provided in the past (Spitze & Logan, 1992; van Tilburg & Broese van Groenou, 2002). Some studies suggest that old people, when too afflicted by health problems to give services, endeavor to make up for that shortcoming by giving greater emotional support (Reinhardt, 2001; van Tilburg, 1998)

In contrast, ADL-independent frail persons were caregivers to the same degree as the robust oldest old. The ADL-independent frail elderly people in our sample maintained the give and take of support in their relationships, even though in some instances certain types of support became increasingly difficult to provide. Qualitative interviews with a subset of Swilsoo participants showed that there was a decrease in some types of services but this was offset by other types of help that could still be performed. The ability to maintain certain levels of support provision when a person is ADL-independent frail may also be influenced by the recourse to the formal network. The latter can help frail people to save time and resources and thus allow them to go on providing services to their family (Baltes & Carstensen, 1996; Künemund & Rein, 1999). The ability to reciprocate the support that older persons receive from their family networks enables them to continue playing a positive role within their family. This continuity of roles may in turn impact positively the well-being of an aged parent (Boerner & Reinhardt, 2003; Krause et al., 1992).

The effects of age and socio-economic status on service exchanges were consistent with the findings of previous research (for instance Boerner & Reinhardt, 2003; van Tilburg & Broese van Groenou, 2002). Being older predicted higher levels of services received and fewer services provided, while persons of middle or upper socio-economic status received fewer services from their family than those of lower status. It may be that those of middle or upper socio-economic status paid for private support instead of relying mainly on their family.

Although there was only a five-year gap between the two sampled cohorts, we found that participants of the first cohort exchanged services more frequently with their family than those of the second. Moreover, persons living in the urban area received and provided services less frequently than those residing in the semi-rural area, where intergenerational solidarity is more developed because of the agricultural culture of the region. In an urban context, a pattern of organization of daily life can be observed which is based on delegation of some domestic chores to paid personnel, whereas in the semi-rural region these tasks are rather performed by relatives (Lalive d'Epinay, Bickel, Maystre, & Vollenwyder, 2000). This geographical effect was less pronounced for individuals of the second cohort. In the space of five years, the differences in socio-economic structure between the two geographical areas had indeed decreased.

In conclusion, the provision of services by very old persons was drastically altered by their individual ADL impairments. The fact that elders affected by frailty maintain the support they provide to their family at the same level as robust elders do is evidence of the importance in old age of preserving a positive and active role within the family. Lastly, the differences in service exchanges between the two sampled cohorts indicate a change in the socio-economic structure over the years.

REFERENCES

Armi, F., Guilley, E., & Lalive d'Epinay, C. (in press). The interface between formal and informal support in advanced old age: A ten-year study. *International Journal of Ageing and Later Life.*

Baltes, M. M., & Carstensen, L. L. (1996). The process of successful ageing. *Ageing and Society, 16*(4), 397-422.

Becker, G., Beyene, Y., Newsom, E., & Mayen, N. (2003). Creating continuity through mutual assistance: Intergenerational reciprocity in four ethnic groups. *Journal of Gerontology: Social Sciences, 58B*(3), S151-S159.

Boerner, K., & Reinhardt, J. P. (2003). Giving while in need: Support provided by disabled older adults. *Journal of Gerontology: Social Sciences, 58B*(5), S297-S304.

Bryk, A. S., & Raudenbush, S. W. (1992). *Hierarchical Linear Models; Applications and data analysis methods*. Newbury Park, CA: Sage Publications.

Guilley, E., Ghisletta, P., Armi, F., Berchtold, A., Lalive d'Epinay, C., Michel, J.-P., et al. (2008). Dynamics of frailty and ADL-dependence in a five-year longitudinal study of octogenarians. *Research on Aging, 30*(3), 299-317.

Katz, S., Ford, A. B., Moskowitz, R. W., Jackson, B. A., & Jaffee, M. W. (1963). Studies of illness in the aged. The index of ADL: A standardized measure of biological and psychosocial function. *Journal of the American Medical Association, 185*, 94-101.

Krause, N. M., Herzog, R. A., & Baker, E. (1992). Providing Support to Others and Well-Being in Later Life. *Journal of Gerontology, 47*(5), P300-P311.

Künemund, H., & Rein, M. (1999). There is more to receiving than needing: Theoretical arguments and empirical explorations of crowding in and crowding out. *Ageing and Society, 19*, 99-121.

Lalive d'Epinay, C., Bickel, J.-F., Maystre, C., & Vollenwyder, N. (2000). *Vieillesses au fil du temps. 1979-1994: une révolution tranquille [Old age across the years. 1979-1994: A quiet revolution]*. Lausanne: Réalités sociales.

Liang, J., Krause, N. M., & Bennett, J. M. (2001). Social exchange and well-being: Is giving better than receiving? *Psychology and Aging, 16*, 511-523.

Raudenbush, S. W., Bryk, A. S., Cheong, Y. F., & Congdon, R. T., Jr. (2004). *HLM 6: Hierarchical Linear and Nonlinear Modelling* (6 ed.). Lincolnwood, IL: Scientific Software International.

Reinhardt, J. P. (2001). Effects of positive and negative support received and provided on adaptation to chronic visual impairment. *Applied Developmental Science, 5*, 76-85.

Spitze, G., & Logan, J. R. (1992). Helping as a component of parent-adult child relations. *Research on aging, 14*(3), 291-312.

van Tilburg, T. (1998). Losing and gaining in old age: Changes in personal network size and social support in a four-year longitudinal study. *Journal of Gerontology: Social Sciences, 53B*(6), S313-S323.

van Tilburg, T., & Broese van Groenou, M. I. (2002). Network and health changes among older Dutch adults. *Journal of Social Issues, 58*(4), 697-713.

Wentowsky, G. J. (1981). Reciprocity and the coping strategies of older people: Cultural dimensions of network building. *The Gerontologist, 21*(6), 600-609.

In: The Closing Chapters of Long Lives
Editors: E. Guilley, Ch. J. Lalive d'Epinay

ISBN: 978-1-60456-971-1

Chapter 7

RETAINING OR RECOVERING ROBUSTNESS IN VERY OLD AGE: WHAT IS THE ROLE OF SOCIAL RELATIONSHIPS?

Franca Armi*[*] *and Edith Guilley

ABSTRACT

This chapter investigates the potential effect of social relationships - composition of social networks and frequency of contacts among family and friendship networks – on whether elders retain or recover their robustness in very old age. Multilevel analyses were used to identify the short-term (12 or 18 months) effects of social relationships on robustness, after controlling for socio-demographic and health-related variables. Our analyses indicated that the existence of siblings had a significant impact on the maintenance or recovery of robustness, which was not the case with the other variables concerning the network composition. Paying visits to the family also had a beneficial effect on this health outcome. Our results highlighted the importance of family relationships in the lives of the oldest old.

---

[*] This chapter is a revised version of an earlier article entitled, "The impact of social relationships on the maintenance of independence in advanced old age: findings of a Swiss longitudinal study", published in the *Zeitschrift für Gerontologie und Geriatrie*, 2005, volume 38, pages 203-209, and based on the first five waves of the first cohort of Swilsoo. We thank the authors Stéphanie Pin, Dario Spini and Christian J. Lalive d'Epinay for their contribution.
Correspondence concerning this chapter should be addressed to Franca Armi, Center for Interdisciplinary Gerontology, Rte de Drize 7, Site Battelle, CH – 1227 Carouge, Switzerland. armif@bluewin.ch

INTRODUCTION

Since the 1980s, gerontology researchers have investigated the psychological and social aspects of aging. While there is strong evidence that social relationships are related to survival, their effects on health remain unclear. Social networks have been proved to delay the onset of frailty (cf. Strawbridge, Shema, Balfour, Higby, & Kaplan, 1998) and of disability (for instance see Giles, Metcalf, Glonek, Luszcz, & Andrews, 2004; Mendes de Leon, Glass, Beckett, Seeman, Evans, & Berkman, 1999). In contrast, other authors have failed to identify any such protective effect on physical functions (e.g. Berkman et al., 1993; Seeman, Bruce, & McAvay, 1996). Furthermore, there has been less research on the question of whether social relationships in very old age are still predictors of health. Bearing in mind that individuals who live into their eighties are generally considered to be different from younger elderly people in that they are "survivors", the role of social relationships on health may differ in late life. Moreover, little work drawing on longitudinal data over an extended period of time has been done on the evolution of social relationships, and yet it is only this kind of research that can bring to light the evolution of social relationships and their effects on health.

In the literature, social networks are divided into two categories - family and friends. The former consists of relationships which are governed by a measure of cultural obligation while the latter is built up from elective choices and is based on reciprocity of exchanges. In this chapter, two dimensions of these two types of social network are studied in connection with health: the composition of the networks, and the frequency of social contacts. A study of the composition of networks involves examining the potential resources available to older people. The circle of people around a very old person tends to change with time: the oldest members (spouse, siblings and contemporary friends) frequently suffer from ill-health or diminished mobility and are more likely to die, while new relatives (grandchildren, great-grandchildren) may become part of the family network and new friendships may be made. But the arrival of new relatives cannot offset the loss of a contemporary because relationships with younger generations have less functional content (Johnson & Barer, 1997). The second dimension relates to the frequency of the contacts older people maintain with members of their family and with friends. Contrary to the belief that individuals become increasingly isolated with advancing age, it is observed that only relationships with distant members of the networks tend to wane; in contrast, contacts with close relatives and confidants remain remarkably stable, even among the oldest old (Pin, Guilley, Lalive d'Epinay, & Vascotto Karkin, 2001). This fits the socio-emotional selectivity theory (Carstensen, 1991), which holds that older people adjust to changes in their situations by restricting their relationships to those which bring them the greatest emotional well-being.

On the basis of data from Swilsoo (Swiss Interdisciplinary Longitudinal Study on the Oldest Old), this chapter investigates the potential effect of social relationships on the maintenance or recovery of robustness in a very old population. More specifically, the nature of that impact is studied in relation to two questions: a) What features of the person's social networks (composition and/or frequency of social contacts) are related to retaining or recovering robustness? b) Which members of a person's network play a major role?

METHODS

Participants

Of the 652 community-dwelling participants making up the two cohorts of Swilsoo, the 479 who answered the questionnaire in person at least at two successive waves (totalling 1,735 interviews across the study) formed the basis of this chapter. Proxy respondents, nursing-home residents and participants assessed only once were excluded (see chapter 1 for a description of the whole sample). The socio-demographic characteristics of the analytical sample closely matched those of the other community-dwelling participants.

Measures

Health was operationalized in three statuses: ADL-dependent, ADL-independent frail, and robust. A participant was considered ADL-dependent if he/she was unable to perform alone at least one of five activities of daily living (washing, dressing and undressing, eating, rising from and going to bed, and moving from one room to another; cf. Katz, Ford, Moskowitz, Jackson, & Jaffee, 1963). Participants without ADL incapacities but suffering from two or more deficiencies in five health domains (sensoriality, mobility, memory, energy, and physical ailments) were considered as ADL-independent frail, and participants without ADL incapacities and with less than two deficiencies in the health domains were considered robust (for further details, see Guilley et al., 2008).

To ascertain the composition of social networks, we noted whether the participant lived alone and whether he/she had at least one child, one sibling or one friend "to whom he/she personally feels very close". Six questions sought information on the frequency (almost never, at least once a year, once a month, once a week, almost daily) of contacts, which could take the form of telephone calls or visits exchanged within the family (not counting spouses or cohabitants) and with friends and/or acquaintances.

The socio-demographic variables used in the present study included age, gender, geographical area (urban or semi-rural) and socio-economic status (working-class or middle/upper-class). Socio-economic status was assessed as a composite of education, income and socio-occupational categories.

Plan of Analysis

Multilevel analyses were used to detect the impact of social relationships on the maintenance or recovery of robustness over a short period (12-18 months). To that end, we calculated the explanatory variables with reference to the time of the wave preceding each measurement of robustness. Age (centered on its grand mean), household composition, composition of social network, health status and the frequency of contacts with family and with friends and/or acquaintances were included as level-1, time-varying predictors, and cohort, gender, socio-economic status, geographical area as level-2, time-invariant predictors. To begin with, we carried out a series of univariate models for each variable we used. We also looked for interaction effects between the above-mentioned factors, but no significant interactions were found. A multivariate analysis was then established, in which the variables that had proved of significance during the selective analyses were included. Multilevel analyses can tolerate an incomplete data set because they use all available data instead of restricting the analysis to individuals who continued to participate up to the end of the follow-up. They therefore limit the selectivity effects. Multilevel models were fitted by the method of restricted maximum likelihood using HLM version 6 (Raudenbush, Bryk, Cheong, & Congdon, 2004) and results were reported with a robust estimation of the standard errors.

Table 1. Characteristics at baseline of the analytical sample (N=479)

Domain	Characteristics	% or mean (SD)
Socio-demographic	Age (years), mean (SD)	81.8 (1.4)
	Cohort (2nd)	53.7
	Gender: woman	49.7
	Socio-economic status: middle/upper-class	49.7
	Geographical area: urban	51.6
Health status	Is robust	48.4
	Is ADL-independent frail	47.4
	Is ADL-dependent	4.2
Household composition	Lives with a cohabitant	55.4
Composition of social network	Has at least one child	80.3
	Has at least one sibling	69.0
	Has at least one close friend	76.3
Contacts with the family (at least once a week)	Receives visits	57.6
	Pays visits	34.0
	Talks on the phone	71.7
Contacts with friends and/or acquaintances (at least once a week)	Receives visits	25.1
	Pays visits	20.3
	Talks on the phone	41.6

RESULTS

At baseline 48.4%, 47.4%, and 4.2% of the sample were classified respectively as robust, ADL-independent frail, and ADL-dependent (Table 1). The low percentage of ADL-dependent participants can be explained by the fact that persons living in nursing-homes and proxy respondents were not taken into account at baseline. Furthermore, the participants benefited from the presence of family and friends: 55.4% lived with a cohabitant, 80.3% had at least one living child, 69.0% one living sibling, and 76.3% at least one close friend. As regards the intensity of social contacts, face-to-face meetings and phone contacts were more frequent within the family network than with the friendship network, as largely demonstrated by other studies (e.g. Broese van Groenou & van Tilburg, 1997). In the family network, paying visits was less frequent than receiving visits (57.6% received visits and 34.0% paid visits weekly), while paying visits (20.3%) was as frequent as receiving visits (25.1%) within the friendship network.

Table 2. Determinants of the maintenance or recovery of robustness over the short term (n = 1,735 interviews)

	Odd Ratio (95% C.I.)	
	Univariate	Multivariate
Socio-demographic		
Cohort (2nd)	1.52 (1.15-2.01)**	1.27 (1.00-1.62)*
Gender: woman	0.59 (0.44-0.78)***	0.62 (0.49-0.79)***
Socio-economic status: middle/upper-class	1.07 (0.81-1.42)	/
Geographical area: urban	1.01 (0.77-1.34)	/
Age (years)	0.85 (0.81-0.89)***	0.90 (0.86-0.94)***
Health status		
Robust *vs* ADL-independent frail	6.49 (5.07-8.31)***	4.51 (3.52-5.78)***
ADL-dependent *vs* ADL-independent frail	0.32 (0.22-0.47)***	0.51 (0.30-0.86)*
Household composition		
Lives with a cohabitant	1.22 (0.95-1.59)	/
Composition of social network		
Has at least one child	1.02 (0.73-1.44)	/
Has at least one sibling	1.43 (1.09-1.88)*	1.28 (1.01-1.63)*
Has at least one close friend	1.17 (0.94-1.44)	/
Frequency of contacts with the family		
Receives visits	0.99 (0.91-1.08)	/
Pays visits	1.25 (1.13-1.37)***	1.20 (1.08-1.32)**
Talks on the phone	1.03 (0.95-1.12)	/
Frequency of contacts with friends and/or acquaintances		
Receives visits	1.03 (0.95-1.11)	/
Pays visits	1.17 (1.08-1.27)***	1.05 (0.96-1.15)
Talks on the phone	1.05 (0.97-1.14)	/

*: $p<0.05$; **: $p<0.01$; ***: $p<0.001$; /: variables not included in multivariate modeling because of their insignificant effects in univariate modeling. Determinants were assessed with reference to the time of the wave preceding each measurement of robustness.

Table 2 shows the chances very old people have of retaining or regaining their robustness in the short term. Present good health was to a considerable degree a function of the previous state of health: robust participants were 4.5 times more likely to remain robust than the ADL-independent frail were to recover their robustness, while the latter were twice as likely to recover their robustness as ADL-dependent participants. The negative effect of age was evident; the oldest persons in the sample being at greater risk of losing their robustness in the short term. Furthermore, men and participants in the second cohort were more likely to maintain or to recover their robustness 12 or 18 months later. The presence of at least one living sibling increased the likelihood of keeping or recovering functional autonomy until the next wave. Lastly, visits paid by the older person to his/her family and to friends and/or acquaintances had a positive effect on robustness over the short term. The other variables bore no univariate relationship to the health outcome. In a multivariate analysis, the above-mentioned effects remained significant except for that of visits paid to friends and/or acquaintances.

Discussion

Using data relating to a very old population followed up over a period of ten years, this chapter sought answers to the following questions: What features of a person's social networks (composition and/or frequency of social contacts) are related to retaining or recovering robustness? Which members of a person's network play a major role?

Paying visits to the family had a beneficial effect on the maintenance or recovery of robustness. It may in fact have the same beneficial effect as providing services (Armi, Guilley, & Lalive d'Epinay, 2008), which enables the older person to continue to play an active role within the family and to maintain the principle of reciprocity. The latter has an impact on well-being, which in turn enhances physical health (Feist, Bodner, Jacobs, Miles, & Tan, 1995). As for the frequency of visits received from the family, it had no effect on robustness. Receiving visits may be associated with both benefits and stress. On the one hand, receiving visits may be interpreted as an anticipated support (i.e. belief that others will provide assistance in case of need). This support has been shown to have a protective effect on health (Shaw & Janevic, 2004). On the other hand, receiving visits, which may imply receiving services, may have a negative effect on health when the family performs tasks for the older person instead of encouraging the person to do so him- or herself (Avlund, Lund, Holstein, Due, Sakari-Rantala, & Heikkinen, 2004).

Before concluding that a child has no influence, it should be recalled that a child has an important role to play in the social life of an aged person and determines to a considerable degree the level of the latter's contacts within the family. This is demonstrated by the association between having a child and receiving or paying visits ($\chi^2 = 479.7$; $p < 0.001$ and $\chi^2 = 168.8$; $p<0.001$, respectively). It is also possible that the weak predictive power of the variable "children" in our study reflects the insensitivity of the measure used: the existence of children may not in itself ensure an emotional link between very old parents and their children. Because they are formally prescribed and governed by cultural obligations and responsibilities, interactions with children do not necessarily imply an emotional dimension (Mullins, Smith, Colquitt, & Mushel, 1996).

Our study revealed that the presence of a brother or sister was related to the chances that a very old person could maintain or recover robustness in the short term. With age, the feeling of closeness to siblings grows stronger (Cicirelli, 1982). Siblings often operate as confidants in old age (Connidis & Davies, 1992) and contribute to the well-being of the elderly (Hilkevitch Bedford, 1995). The confidant, as the principal source of well-being, appears to reduce the psychological consequences of stress on functional health, for instance, by increasing self-esteem or facilitating the establishment of adaptive strategies (House, Landis, & Umberson, 1988; Krause & Borawski-Clark, 1994; Siegrist, 2000). A second interpretation would be that the "sibling" effect reflects a genetic influence: those still having surviving siblings may belong to high-longevity and healthy families. One study based on identical and fraternal twins supports the genetic hypothesis, suggesting the significant influence of genetic effects on variations in longevity (Ljungquist, Berg, Lanke, McClearn, & Pedersen, 1998).

The impact of the friendship network, and particularly of the confidant, in matters relating to mortality (Guilley, Pin, Spini, Lalive d'Epinay, Herrmann, & Michel, 2005; Johnson & Barer, 1997) and psychological well-being (Bowling & Browne, 1991; Seeman et al., 1996), has been demonstrated. In contrast, in matters relating to robustness the situation is less clear; although over the long term the friendship network does not seem to determine functional health (Seeman et al., 1996), other studies find that friendship contacts do affect the development of disabilities and recovery in the short term (Mendes de Leon et al., 1999; Oxman & Hull, 1997). Our multivariate analysis showed that contacts with friends and/or acquaintances and the presence of a close friend had no impact on the maintenance or recovery of robustness. We wonder if the very old tend to give contacts with their family preference over those with friends in order to preserve their resources (this ability to preserve resources would be at tune with the theory of socio-emotional selectivity; cf. Carstensen, 1991). The family would therefore become the favoured source of emotional support (e.g. Broese van Groenou & van Tilburg, 1997). It should also be remembered that friends are usually contemporaries of the very old and therefore frequently suffer from ill-health or diminished mobility.

Apart from those social determinants, other factors were found to play a role in the maintenance or recovery of robustness. The strongest factor favouring a healthy trajectory was the health status during the preceding wave: the chances of retaining or recovering robustness decreased drastically with worsening health status. Robust participants were very likely to maintain their robustness while the chances for the ADL-independent frail to recover their robustness were poorer but not negligible (for the exact percentages, see chapter 2, Table 1). In spite of their shorter life expectancy, men were more likely than women to retain or recover their robustness. This gender paradox is well known in the literature; it may be of biological origin but may also be socially constructed (e.g. lower level of education and income for women) by being linked to gender roles (e.g. greater likelihood for women to be caregivers) (Arber & Cooper, 1999; Moen & Spencer, 2006). Lastly, we found that participants in the second cohort (born five years later), who were initially in better health (cf. chapter 2), were more likely to retain or recover their robustness. This health improvement between successive generations had been shown by other studies (e.g. Lalive d'Epinay, Bickel, Maystre, & Vollenwyder, 2000; Manton, Singer, & Suzman, 1993; Waidmann & Manton, 2000). The causes of this health improvement are likely to be multiple and to include healthier lifestyles and advances in medicine (Fries, 2005; Hubert, Bloch, Oehlert, & Fries, 2002).

In conclusion, our analyses have demonstrated that social relationships have an impact on robustness. Visits paid to the family and the presence of a sibling favoured the maintenance or recovery of good health. Both features of the person's social networks (composition and/or frequency of social contacts) consequently played a role in health outcomes. Our results highlight the importance of family relationships in the lives of the oldest old. The ability of older persons to continue playing an active role by paying visits to their family enhances their well-being and may in turn help them to retain or recover their robustness.

REFERENCES

Arber, S., & Cooper, H. (1999). Gender differences in health in later life: The new paradox? *Social Sciences and Medicine, 48*, 61-76.

Armi, F., Guilley, E., & Lalive d'Epinay, C. (2008). Health: Support provided and received in advanced old age. A five-years follow-up. *Zeitschrift für Gerontologie und Geriatrie, 41*, 56-62.

Avlund, K., Lund, R., Holstein, B. E., Due, P., Sakari-Rantala, R., & Heikkinen, R.-L. (2004). The impact of structural and functional characteristics of social relations as determinants of functional decline. *Journal of Gerontology: Social Sciences, 59B*(1), S44-S51.

Berkman, L. F., Seeman, T. E., Albert, M. S., Blazer, D. G., Kahn, R. L., Mohs, R., et al. (1993). High, usual, and impaired functioning in community-dwelling older men and women: Findings from the MacArthur Foundation Research Network on Successful Aging. *Journal of Clinical Gerontology, 46*, 1129-1140.

Bowling, A., & Browne, P. D. (1991). Social networks, health and emotional well-being among the oldest old in London. *Journal of Gerontology, 46*(1), S20-S32.

Broese van Groenou, M. I., & van Tilburg, T. (1997). Changes in the support networks of older adults in the Netherlands. *Journal of Cross-Cultural Gerontology, 12*(1), 23-44.

Carstensen, L. L. (1991). Selectivity theory: Social activity in life-span context. *Annual Review of Gerontology and Geriatrics, 11*, 195-217.

Cicirelli, V. G. (1982). Sibling influence throughout the lifespan. In M. E. Lamb, & B. Sutton-Smith (Eds.), *Sibling relationships: their nature and significance across the lifespan*. Hillsdale, NJ: Lawrence Erlbaum.

Connidis, I. A., & Davies, L. (1992). Confidants and companions: Choices in later life. *Journal of Gerontology, 47*(3), S115-S122.

Feist, G. J., Bodner, T. E., Jacobs, J. F., Miles, M., & Tan, V. (1995). Integrating top-down and bottom-up structural models of subjective well-being: A longitudinal investigation. *Journal of Personality and Social Psychology, 68*(1), 138-150.

Fries, J. F. (2005). Frailty, heart disease, and stroke. The compression of morbidity paradigm. *American Journal of Preventive Medicine, 29*, 164-168.

Giles, L. C., Metcalf, P. A., Glonek, G. F. V., Luszcz, M. A., & Andrews, G. R. (2004). The effect of social networks on disability in older Australians. *Journal of Aging and Health, 16*(4), 517-538.

Guilley, E., Ghisletta, P., Armi, F., Berchtold, A., Lalive d'Epinay, C., Michel, J.-P., et al. (2008). Dynamics of frailty and ADL-dependence in a five-year longitudinal study of octogenarians. *Research on Aging, 30*(3), 299-317.

Guilley, E., Pin, S., Spini, D., Lalive d'Epinay, C., Herrmann, F. R., & Michel, J.-P. (2005). Association between social relationships and survival of Swiss octogenarians. A five-year prospective, population-based study. *Aging Clinical and Experimental Research, 17*(5), 419-425.

Hilkevitch Bedford, V. (1995). Sibling relationships in middle and old age. In R. Blieszner, & V. Hilkevitch Bedford (Eds.), *Handbook of aging and the family* (pp. 201-222). Westport: Greenwood Press.

House, J. S., Landis, K. R., & Umberson, D. (1988). Social relationships and health. *Science, 241*, 540-545.

Hubert, H. B., Bloch, D. A., Oehlert, J. W., & Fries, J. F. (2002). Lifestyle habits and compression of morbidity. *Journal of Gerontology: Medical Sciences, 57A*(6), 347-351.

Johnson, C. L., & Barer, B. M. (1997). *Life beyond 85 years. The aura of survivorship*. New York: Springer.

Katz, S., Ford, A. B., Moskowitz, R. W., Jackson, B. A., & Jaffee, M. W. (1963). Studies of illness in the aged. The index of ADL: A standardized measure of biological and psychosocial function. *Journal of the American Medical Association, 185*, 94-101.

Krause, N. M., & Borawski-Clark, E. (1994). Clarifying the functions of social support in later life. *Research on Aging, 16*(3), 251-279.

Lalive d'Epinay, C., Bickel, J.-F., Maystre, C., & Vollenwyder, N. (2000). *Vieillesses au fil du temps. 1979-1994: une révolution tranquille [Old age across the years. 1979-1994: A quiet revolution]*. Lausanne: Réalités sociales.

Ljungquist, B., Berg, S., Lanke, J., McClearn, G. E., & Pedersen, N. L. (1998). The effect of genetic factors for longevity: A comparison of identical and fraternal twins in the Swedish Twin Registry. *Journal of Gerontology: Biological Sciences, 53A*, 441-446.

Manton, K. G., Singer, B. H., & Suzman, R. M. (1993). *Forecasting the health of elderly populations*. New York: Springer-Verlag.

Mendes de Leon, C. F., Glass, T. A., Beckett, L. A., Seeman, T. E., Evans, D. A., & Berkman, L. F. (1999). Social networks and disability transitions across eight intervals of yearly data in the New Haven EPESE. *Journal of Gerontology: Social Sciences, 54B*(3), S162-S172.

Moen, P., & Spencer, D. (2006). Converging Divergences in Age, Gender, Health, and Well-Being: Strategic Selection in the Third Age. In L. K. George, & R. H. Binstock (Eds.), *Handbook of aging and the social sciences* (6th ed., pp. 127-144). Amsterdam: Elsevier.

Mullins, L. C., Smith, R., Colquitt, R., & Mushel, M. (1996). An examination of the effects of self-rated and objective indicators of health condition and economic condition on the loneliness of older persons. *Journal of Applied Gerontology, 15*, 23-37.

Oxman, T. E., & Hull, J. G. (1997). Social support, depression and activities of daily living in older heart surgery patients. *Journal of Gerontology: Social Sciences, 52B*, 1-14.

Pin, S., Guilley, E., Lalive d'Epinay, C., & Vascotto Karkin, B. (2001). La dynamique de la vie familiale et amicale durant la vieillesse [Dynamics of the family and friendship networks during the very old age]. *Gérontologie et Société, 98*, 85-101.

Raudenbush, S. W., Bryk, A. S., Cheong, Y. F., & Congdon, R. T., Jr. (2004). *HLM 6: Hierarchical Linear and Nonlinear Modelling* (6 ed.). Lincolnwood, IL: Scientific Software International.

Seeman, T. E., Bruce, M. L., & McAvay, G. J. (1996). Social network characteristics and onset of ADL disability: MacArthur Studies of Successful Aging. *Journal of Gerontology: Social Sciences, 51B*, S191-S200.

Shaw, B. A., & Janevic, M. (2004). Association between anticipated support, physical functionning, and education level among a nationally representative sample of older adults. *Journal of Aging and Health, 16*(4), 539-561.

Siegrist, J. (2000). The social causation of health and illness. In G. L. Albrecht, R. Fitzpatrick, & S. C. Scrimshaw (Eds.), *The handbook of social studies in health and medicine* (pp. 100-114). London: Sage.

Strawbridge, W. J., Shema, S. J., Balfour, J. L., Higby, H. R., & Kaplan, G. A. (1998). Antecedents of frailty over three decades in an older cohort. *Journal of Gerontology: Social Sciences, 53B*, S9-S16.

Waidmann, T. A., & Manton, K. G. (2000). *Measuring trends in availability among the elderly: An international review.* Washington DC: Urban Institute.

In: The Closing Chapters of Long Lives
Editors: E. Guilley, Ch. J. Lalive d'Epinay

ISBN: 978-1-60456-971-1

Chapter 8

THE INTERFACE BETWEEN FORMAL AND INFORMAL SUPPORT: DOES FORMAL SUPPORT SUBSTITUTE INFORMAL ONE?*

Franca Armi*†*, Edith Guilley, and Christian J. Lalive d'Epinay

ABSTRACT

The aim of this paper is to investigate the interface between the formal and informal support provided to very old people against a background of increasing need for care and a decreasing number of potential informal caregivers. We used a sample of 323 community-dwelling octogenarians participating in the Swiss Interdisciplinary Longitudinal Study on the Oldest Old (Swilsoo) (n = 1441 interviews). Descriptive analyses and a multilevel model were used to test whether formal and informal services complemented or substituted one another. The study revealed that the amount of informal services increased significantly as the frequency of formal aid increased, indicating that the two networks were complementary in the majority of the cases. In 21.2% of the cases, the formal network partly substituted the informal network (as an adjustment) and only in 6.4% of the cases did the informal support end after the formal support had increased (radical substitution). The concern that the introduction of formal services may curb the readiness of relatives and friends to provide care is thus unfounded.

* This work is already electronically published at IJAL (International Journal of Ageing and Later Life). The authors have retained the copyright for their work published at IJAL.

† Correspondence concerning this chapter should be addressed to Franca Armi, Center for Interdisciplinary Gerontology, Rte de Drize 7, Site Battelle, CH – 1227 Carouge, Switzerland. armif@bluewin.ch

INTRODUCTION

Since the 1980's, the relationship between formal and informal support networks has been widely studied. Nevertheless, how the two networks coexist continues to present researchers with numerous conceptual challenges. Various theoretical models have been devised to describe the interface between formal and informal services (cf. Davey & Patsios, 1999; Travis, 1995; Vézina & Membrado, 2005). The substitution model hypothesizes that formal services replace part of the support provided by informal networks. It thus implies a negative correlation between the evolution of formal and informal services. According to the substitution model, the introduction of formal services may prompt relatives and friends to curtail their informal caregiving efforts and curb their feeling of responsibility for care. In contrast to the substitution model, the complementary and supplemental models hypothesize that the introduction of formal services does not induce a significant drop in the amount of services provided by the informal networks. By applying a task-oriented approach, the latter two models can be differentiated: in a complementary arrangement, one given task is performed by both networks while in a supplemental arrangement, some tasks are performed by both networks while others are specifically performed by one or the other network. Lastly, the hierarchical compensatory model details older adults' hierarchical preference for assistance. Elders are more likely to look first to spouses, next to adult children, then to other relatives and friends, and finally to formal services for support. The last-mentioned generally come into play solely when no informal network is available (Cantor, 1979).

Previous studies on the relationship between formal and informal networks relied mainly on cross-sectional data (e.g. Davey & Patsios, 1999; Penning, 2002; Sundström, Malmberg, & Johansson, 2006). While cross-sectional studies are very informative with respect to care utilisation differences between individuals, only longitudinal data can throw light on the effect of changes in the formal network on the amount of informal social support. In order to study the interface between formal and informal networks, longitudinal data are thus required. Furthermore, the previous studies mentioned above were essentially devoted to the younger elderly. For this population, empirical evidence of the substitution hypothesis was seldom documented (cf. for instance Logan & Spitze, 1994). The substitution was found to occur only over the short term (Tennstedt, Harrow, & Crawford, 1996) and therefore tended to be temporary. To our knowledge, no study has examined the formal-informal interface specifically among a very old population. This population needs more assistance with personal care than the younger elderly and therefore lends itself to a study of the relationship between formal and informal networks. Cases of substitution may be more frequent in a very old population when contemporary caregivers are also very old and are likely to have assumed the role of caregiver for a long time.

Our objective was to investigate the formal-informal interface in the context of an increasing need for care and a decreasing number of potential informal carers, within a population of Swiss octogenarians monitored over a period of ten years. In other words, we wanted to see how help from informal networks evolves when the utilisation of formal services increases. We tested the following three models: (1) complementary: the increase in formal support is associated with an increase in, or stability of, informal support; (2) substitution as an adjustment in the informal network: the increase in formal support is associated with a relative decline in informal aid; and (3) radical substitution: the increase in formal support is associated with the disappearance of informal aid. It was impossible to differentiate the complementary model from the supplemental one, because we did not ask who provided help with each of the tasks considered.

METHODS

Participants

Analyses from the Swilsoo were limited to the 323 participants who provided sufficient data for computation (see Table 1 for the number of participants at each wave). The octogenarians answered a trained interviewer, either in person or, if unable to do so, through a proxy (the proportion of proxy reports ranged from 8.7% to 26.2% in the course of the study period). After the ten-year period, there were 59 (18.3%) surviving participants (of whom 45 were still community-dwellers) and 37 (11.4%) surviving dropouts, while 227 (70.3%) of the original participants had died.

Measures

We defined informal support as the help received from family members and friends and/or acquaintances, excluding help received from household members. Two series of questions assessed the frequency of six instrumental aids[1] that the very old person received from such sources. A choice of four possible answers was given: "never", "rarely", "sometimes", and "often". All community-dwelling participants were questioned. For the formal network, which is provided by subsidized or fee-paid professionals, a series of six types of service[2] was put to all community-dwelling participants, with six possible answers: "never", "rarely", "every month", "every two weeks", "once a week", "every day". Those questions enabled us to construct frequency scores for each of the three networks (family, friends and formal) by averaging out the different answers given. The mean frequency scores for family members and for friends and/or acquaintances were merged to obtain a score for the non-household informal services.

The formal-informal care interface was analyzed with controls of potential confounding factors such as socio-demographic variables, need factors, and household and informal network composition.

---

1 Performing household tasks; bringing or preparing meals; doing the shopping; doing repairs, odd jobs and gardening; help with completing income tax returns and insurance claims; help with toilet activities

2 Care from a nurse; help from a household/family helper (with everyday tasks such as housework, washing, shopping, preparing meals, and going to see the doctor); counselling from a social worker (for example, to help complete formalities, fill in forms, apply for aid from other agencies, manage his/her money); home-delivered meals; day-care or voluntary centres; help from an association. (Various associations such as Pro Senectute offer services to older people. The associations' staff and volunteers deliver such services as social counselling, the provision of practical information, and assistance in arranging home help, and in addition make available a range of suitable activities.) The services most used were household/family helper and care from a nurse.

Table 1. Number of interviews with the community-dwelling participants across the nine waves of Swilsoo

	Waves									
	1	*2*	*3*	*4*	*5*	*6*	*7*	*8*	*9*	*Total*
Self-respondents	*295*	*224*	*190*	*162*	*124*	*99*	*75*	*51*	*42*	*1262*
Proxy respondents	*28*	*27*	*29*	*28*	*29*	*16*	*10*	*9*	*3*	*176*
Total	*323*	*251*	*219*	*190*	*153*	*115*	*85*	*60*	*45*	*1441*

The socio-demographic variables used were age, gender, geographical area (urban or semi-rural area) and socio-economic status (working-class or middle/upper-class). Socio-economic status was assessed as a composite of education, income and socio-occupational categories.

Need factors were assessed by means of a three-tier health status: ADL-dependent, ADL-independent frail, and robust. A participant was considered ADL-dependent if he/she was unable to perform alone at least one of five activities of daily living (washing, dressing and undressing, eating, rising from and going to bed, and moving from one room to another; cf. Katz, Ford, Moskowitz, Jackson, & Jaffee, 1963). Participants having no ADL incapacities but suffering from two or more deficiencies in five health domains (sensoriality, mobility, memory, energy and physical ailments) were considered as ADL-independent frail; participants without ADL incapacities and with less that two deficiencies in the above-mentioned health domains were considered robust (for more details, see Guilley et al., 2008). Swilsoo publications had already demonstrated that each health status was associated with a specific "everyday life-world" (specific well-being, social activities and relationships as well as different risks of adverse health outcomes) (Lalive d'Epinay & Guilley, 2007).

Although this paper deals with the services provided by non-household caregivers, the household composition (living or not with a cohabitant) was taken as a control in the analysis of the formal-informal care interface.

Lastly, the composition of the informal network was assessed by means of standard questions about the existence of living siblings, descendants (children, grandchildren or great grandchildren), and close friends.

Plan of Analysis

Before analyzing the interface between the two networks, we assessed how the need for care and the composition of the informal network evolved over the study period. Multilevel analyses were used to assess the relationship between (a) the need for care or the composition of the informal network and (b) the age of participants. The regression coefficients (β) indicate whether the need for care or the percentage of persons having potential caregivers increases ($\beta > 0$), decreases ($\beta < 0$) or stays the same (β not significantly different from zero) across the study. Analyses were performed on 323 participants (representing 1441 interviews across the nine-wave follow-up). Multilevel analyses were developed for the purpose of analyzing data with multilevel sets (e.g. repeated measures within an individual). They allow the use of repeated measures where both the number of interviews per participant and the time intervals between interviews vary. Furthermore, multilevel analyses can tolerate an incomplete data set because they use all available data (instead of restricting the analysis to individuals who participated in the nine waves of the study) and therefore limit the selectivity effects (Raudenbush & Bryk, 2002; Snijders & Bosker, 1999).

We then tested whether formal and informal networks substitute one another or are complementary. We evaluated the relationship between the frequencies of formal and informal care by using a multilevel analysis on 1441 interviews controlled by socio-demographic variables, need factors and the composition of informal networks. The substitution model implies a negative relationship between formal and informal services while an insignificant or positive relationship is expected in the complementary model. Age (centered on its grand mean), household composition, variables on the presence of an informal network, health status and the frequency of formal care were included as level-1, time-varying predictors, and gender, socio-economic status, and geographical area as level-2, time-invariant predictors. Multilevel models were fitted by the method of restricted maximum likelihood using HLM version 6 (Raudenbush, Bryk, Cheong, & Congdon, 2004) and results were reported with a robust estimation of the standard errors.

Work carried out previously was useful in assessing the relationship between the amount of informal and formal supports, with control of variables, but it gave only general information on the formal-informal care interface. To clarify this interface we adopted a different approach: we examined the proportion of interviews (one individual can be represented more than once) whose pattern of support was consistent with each theoretical model of formal-informal interface. To assess the exact percentage of cases falling into the categories of complementary (increase or stability of the informal network), substitution as an adjustment or radical substitution, we used the following analysis. When the frequency of formal services increased at two successive waves (i.e. periods between waves 1-2, 2-3, and so on), we counted the number of cases for which the frequency of informal services simultaneously (a) increased, (b) stayed the same, (c) decreased, or (d) ceased. This analysis was limited to 236 interviews (those for which one of the two networks was lacking and those presenting no increase in formal help were thus excluded).

RESULTS

Table 2 reports the characteristics of the sample and Table 3 their evolution over the ten-year period. While 60.8% of the participants lived with a cohabitant at baseline, this percentage fell during the study, illustrating the growing number of single people in need of non-household care. The vast majority of very old participants had the benefit of a potential informal network (97.5% at baseline had at least one potential caregiver: a descendant, a sibling or a close friend). However, the network composed of siblings and friends, who were likely to be the participants' contemporaries, shrank over the period. In parallel to those changes, the need for care increased. At baseline, only 9.3% of the persons interviewed were ADL-dependent, 51.6% were ADL-independent frail while 39.1% were still robust in spite of their age. During the study period, the proportion of robust individuals fell sharply while that of ADL-dependent subjects rose.

Table 2. Characteristics at baseline (N=323)

	N (%) [1]
Household composition	
Lives with a cohabitant	*194 (60.8)*
Potential informal network	
Has at least one descendant	*263 (81.4)*
Has at least one sibling	*227 (70.7)*
Has at least one close friend [2]	*213 (73.2)*
Need of care	
Is robust	*126 (39.1)*
Is ADL-independent frail	*166 (51.6)*
Is ADL-dependent	*30 (9.3)*

[1] Percentages are given for subjects without missing values.
[2] Only self-respondents included.

Table 3. Evolution across the nine Swilsoo waves (n = 1441 interviews)

	Evolution across the nine waves [1]*: β (SE)*
Household composition	
Lives with a cohabitant	*-0.05 (0.02)***
Potential informal network	
Has at least one descendant	*0.01 (0.01)*
Has at least one sibling	*-0.09 (0.02)****
Has at least one close friend [2]	*-0.07 (0.02)***
Need of care	
Robust vs ADL-independent frail	*-0.12 (0.02)****
ADL-dependent vs ADL-independent frail	*0.19 (0.03)****

* $p<0.05$, ** $p<0.01$, *** $p<0.001$.
[1] β: unstandardized regression coefficient between the characteristics listed and the age of participants estimated by multilevel analyses.
[2] Only self-respondents included.

Table 4 shows how the help provided by non-household informal services evolved in relation to changes in formal help, with controls for socio-demographic variables, need factors, and household and informal network composition. As could be expected, having one or more descendants substantially increased the frequency of the informal services. Persons living with a cohabitant – who, when present, is often the principal caregiver – received fewer services from the other caregivers. Irrespective of their living arrangements, women were better provided with informal care. The region of residence and the socio-economic status were also determining factors in receiving informal services: persons living in the urban area and persons in the middle and upper socio-economic groups received fewer services. ADL-dependent participants received more informal services than ADL-independent frail persons, who received an amount of services similar to robust persons (previous work has shown that, without controlling for frequency of formal care, persons having different health statuses received different amounts of help, at least among younger old participants). In contrast, the frequency of aid offered by the informal network was the same for both ADL-independent frail and robust persons, at a fixed frequency of formal care. The results also showed that on average the amount of informal services rose in line with increasing frequency of formal aid, thus lending weight to the complementary model. For the oldest ADL-dependent participants, the relationship between formal and informal networks remained positive but was less marked.

As the above analysis yielded only general information on the formal-informal care interface, we assessed the proportion of cases whose pattern of support was consistent with the complementary and substitution (radical or as an adjustment) models. Table 5 presents the changes in the frequency of informal services between two successive waves when the frequency of formal services increased. A greater use of formal services was associated with increased informal care in 47.0% of the interviews, with unchanged intensity of informal care in 25.4% of the interviews, with less extensive informal care in 21.2% of the interviews and with the end of informal services in 6.4% of the interviews. The two networks were hence complementary in 72.4% of the interviews and the formal network substituted (radically or as an adjustment) the informal network in 27.6% of the interviews.

Table 4. Frequency of non-household informal services as a function of the frequency of formal care and controls: multilevel analysis (n = 1441 interviews)

	Unstandardized regression coefficient β (SE)
Socio-demographic	
Age (years)	*0.00 (0.00)*
Gender (woman)	*0.06 (0.03)**
Socio-economic status (middle/upper-class)	*-0.05 (0.02)**
Geographical area (urban)	*-0.10 (0.02)****
Household composition	
Lives with a cohabitant	*-0.10 (0.03)***
Potential informal network	
Has at least one descendant	*0.11 (0.02)****
Has at least one sibling	*0.01 (0.02)*
Has at least one close friend	*0.00 (0.01)*
Need of care	
Robust vs ADL-independent frail	*-0.02 (0.02)*
ADL-dependent vs ADL-independent frail	*2.01 (0.10)**
*Age*ADL-dependent*	*-0.02 (0.01)**
Formal network	
Frequency of formal care	*0.08 (0.02)****

* p<0.05, ** p<0.01, *** p<0.001.

Table 5. Changes in the frequency of informal services between two successive waves when the frequency of formal services increases, number of interviews (%)

Changes in the frequency of informal services between two successive waves	*Complementary*	
	Increase	*111 (47.0)*
	No change	*60 (25.4)*
	Substitution as an adjustment	
	Decrease	*50 (21.2)*
	Radical substitution	
	Cessation	*15 (6.4)*

'Successive waves' means periods between waves 1-2, 2-3, and so on.

Discussion

This study, based on data obtained by monitoring a sample of octogenarians over a period of ten years, was mainly motivated by the following question: in parallel to an increasing need for help and a dwindling number of potential informal helpers, does the help provided by formal services partly replace the informal support? We found that formal and informal supports were on the whole positively related, thus lending weight to the complementary model. By testing three models (complementary, substitution as an adjustment, and radical substitution), we found that the formal and informal networks were complementary in the majority of cases (72.4%). Our results are in harmony with most previous research based on younger old persons, which demonstrated that formal and informal networks were complementary resources (e.g. Davey & Patsios, 1999; Denton, 1997; Penning, 2002). We showed further that additional needs were catered for by formal networks in 25.4% of the cases and by both networks in 47.0%. However, the formal network substituted the informal services in 27.6% of the cases. In 21.2% of the cases, there was an adjustment and only in 6.4% of the cases was there a radical substitution. In the cases of adjustment, the reduction of the informal services was probably a sign that an old parent who had become more severely impaired needed professional care which could no longer be provided by the relatives. Indeed, the informal network tends to continue caring for old persons as long as it is capable of doing so, with formal networks coming into play essentially when professional skills are necessary (Armi, Guilley, & Lalive d'Epinay, 2008). The introduction of formal networks may then lighten the task of the caregivers or redirect them to other forms of care. For the instances of radical substitution (6.4%), two hypotheses are possible. The first would be to postulate a disengagement, which may occur in the case of caregivers for whom the help has become too burdensome. However results from previous research indicate that the disengagement of caregivers is a rare occurrence (e.g. Garant & Bolduc, 1990) even after the institutionalization of a dependent parent, where families continue to provide a high level of help (Cavalli, 2002), or in generous welfare systems, which foster rather than undermine family solidarity (Künemund & Rein, 1999). The second hypothesis could relate to situations where a caregiver had died or had serious health problems.

We also observed the determinants of informal network use which may influence the interface between formal and informal support. Our results are consistent with previous studies which found that women and persons with a lower socio-economic status received more help from the informal network (e.g. Broese van Groenou, Glaser, Tomassini, & Jacobs, 2006; Litwin, 2004). This gender effect may be explained by the fact that women receive less support from their husbands (Gurung, Taylor, & Seeman, 2003), partly because they tend to outlive their husbands and thus are more likely to resort to the non-household informal network. As for the effect of socio-economic status, the relative neediness of persons in the lower-status category prompts more informal help than that given to persons of a higher socio-economic status (Broese van Groenou et al., 2006). We also found that persons living in the semi-rural area received more informal services than the city-dwellers. Indeed, in a semi-rural socio-cultural context, 'being together' tends to imply the sharing of domestic chores and the exchange of services, while in an urban context it implies rather the sharing of a leisure activity (Lalive d'Epinay, Bickel, Maystre, & Vollenwyder, 2000).

In spite of its major strengths (longitudinal design and long-term tracking of very old persons who displayed widely different health statuses), this study was limited by the lack of information on the services provided by the cohabitant, who is likely to be the primary kin caregiver. However this limitation obviously does not concern older persons living alone, who represented half of the sample from the fifth wave onwards. For persons living with their spouse, the amount of help provided by the latter is likely to decrease with time and with advancing age. Those couples may then require more help from non-household caregivers.

Conclusion

This study showed that, in a context of increasing need for care and a declining number of potential informal caregivers, informal and formal networks of support for the very old were complementary in the majority of the cases. Cases of radical substitution were rare. The concern that the introduction of formal services may curb the readiness of relatives and friends to provide care is thus unfounded. Future research should examine how formal networks could share knowledge with informal networks and how the former can act to better support stressed informal caregivers, especially when the latter are also very old and have assumed their role of caregiver for a long time.

References

Armi, F., Guilley, E., & Lalive d'Epinay, C. (2008). Entraide et recours aux services [Mutual assistance and use of services]. In C. Lalive d'Epinay, & D. Spini (Eds.), *Les années fragiles: la vie au-delà des quatre-vingts ans [The frailty years: life beyond eighty years old]* (pp. 209-246). Québec, Canada: Les Presses de l'Université de Laval.

Broese van Groenou, M. I., Glaser, K., Tomassini, C., & Jacobs, T. (2006). Socio-economic status differences in older people's use of informal and formal help: A comparison of four European countries. *Ageing and Society, 26*(5), 745-766.

Cantor, M. H. (1979). Neighbours and friends, an overlooked resource in the informal support system. *Research on Aging, 1*(4), 434-463.

Cavalli, S. (2002). *Vieillards à domicile, vieillards en pension: une comparaison [Elderly at home, elderly in a nursing home: a comparison]*. Lausanne: Réalités Sociales

Davey, A., & Patsios, D. (1999). Formal and informal community care to older adults: Comparative analysis of the United States and Great Britain. *Journal of Family and Economic Issues, 20*(3), 271-299.

Denton, M. (1997). The linkages between informal and formal care of the elderly. *Canadian Journal on Aging, 16*(1), 30-50.

Garant, L., & Bolduc, M. (1990). *L'aide par les proches: Mythes et réalités*. Québec: Direction de l'évaluation, ministère de la santé et des services sociaux.

Guilley, E., Ghisletta, P., Armi, F., Berchtold, A., Lalive d'Epinay, C., Michel, J.-P., et al. (2008). Dynamics of frailty and ADL-dependence in a five-year longitudinal study of octogenarians. *Research on Aging, 30*(3), 299-317.

Gurung, R., A. R., Taylor, S. E., & Seeman, T. E. (2003). Accounting for changes in social support among married older adults: Insights from the MacArthur studies of successful aging. *Psychology and Aging, 18*(3), 487-496.

Katz, S., Ford, A. B., Moskowitz, R. W., Jackson, B. A., & Jaffee, M. W. (1963). Studies of illness in the aged. The index of ADL: A standardized measure of biological and psychosocial function. *Journal of the American Medical Association, 185*(Sep 21), 914-919.

Künemund, H., & Rein, M. (1999). There is more to receiving than needing: Theoretical arguments and empirical explorations of crowding in and crowding out. *Ageing and Society, 19*(1), 99-121.

Lalive d'Epinay, C., Bickel, J.-F., Maystre, C., & Vollenwyder, N. (2000). *Vieillesses au fil du temps. 1979-1994: Une révolution tranquille [Old age across the years. 1979-1994: A quiet revolution]*. Lausanne: Réalités sociales.

Lalive d'Epinay, C., & Guilley, E. (2007). Statuts de santé et mondes de vie quotidienne des vieillards [Health statuses and everyday life-worlds among oldest-old people]. *Swiss Journal of Sociology, 32*(3), 407-427.

Litwin, H. (2004). Social networks, ethnicity and public home-care utilisation. *Ageing and Society, 24*(6), 921-939.

Logan, J. R., & Spitze, G. (1994). Informal support and the use of formal services by older Americans. *Journal of Gerontology, 49*(1), S25-S34.

Penning, M. J. (2002). Hydra revisited: Substituting formal for self- and informal in-home care among older adults with disabilities. *The Gerontologist, 42*(1), 4-16.

Raudenbush, S. W., & Bryk, A. S. (2002). *Hierarchical linear models. Applications and data analysis methods* (2nd ed.). Thousand Oaks: Sage

Raudenbush, S. W., Bryk, A. S., Cheong, Y. F., & Congdon, R. T., Jr. (2004). *HLM 6: Hierarchical Linear and Nonlinear Modelling* (6th ed.). Lincolnwood, IL: Scientific Software International.

Snijders, T. A. B., & Bosker, R. J. (1999). *Multilevel analysis. An introduction to basic and advanced multilevel modeling*. London: Sage.

Sundström, G., Malmberg, B., & Johansson, L. (2006). Balancing family and state care: Neither, either or both? The case of Sweden. *Ageing and Society, 26*(5), 767-782.

Tennstedt, S. L., Harrow, B., & Crawford, S. (1996). Informal care vs. formal services: Changes in patterns of care over time. *Journal of Aging and Social Policy, 7*(3-4), 71-91.

PART 4: PRESERVING WELL-BEING

In: The Closing Chapters of Long Lives
Editors: E. Guilley, Ch. J. Lalive d'Epinay

ISBN: 978-1-60456-971-1

Chapter 9

REMAINING ACTIVE: A BOOST FOR WELL-BEING?

Jean-François Bickel[*] and Myriam Girardin

ABSTRACT

This chapter seeks to gauge the extent to which the continuity of leisure activities can counter the negative effects of frailty on well-being. The cognitive and affective dimensions of well-being are both taken into consideration. Two trajectories of frailty taking place between two successive waves are examined: (a) the onset of frailty and (b) the aggravation of the condition. For both trajectories, the level of activity – continuity versus decline – is monitored over the same period of time. Three profiles are thus defined and compared with one another: health stability (profile I); health deterioration with continuing activity (profile II); health deterioration with activity decline (profile III). For three of the four cases analyzed (two constituents of well-being x two trajectories of frailty), the analyses show that profile II is associated with no significant decline in well-being whose level at the end of the trajectory is very close to that of profile I whereas profile III engenders a marked decline in well-being. These results emphasize that continuity ain leisure activities moderates the negative effects on well-being of the onset and aggravation of frailty and they are on the whole consistent with the theoretical model of continuity.

INTRODUCTION

The practice of leisure activities that are meaningful for the individual has long been regarded as an essential ingredient of the quality of life and well-being in old age. The underlying mechanisms refer us back to the role played by activities in strengthening subjective identity, together with such elements of that identity as the feeling of control and

[*] Correspondence concerning this chapter should be addressed to Jean-François Bickel, University of Fribourg, Department of Social Work and Social Policy, Rte. des Bonnesfontaines 11, CH-1700 Fribourg; jean-francois.bickel@unifr.ch

self-esteem. The postulate was originally formalized as *activity theory*, which claims that, by engaging in an active lifestyle, the elderly can combat the loss of occupational, social or conjugal (through loss of spouse) roles that accompanies retirement and ageing, as well as the adverse effects of such losses on well-being (Havighurst, Neugarten, & Tobin, 1968; Lemon, Bengtson, & Peterson, 1972; Longino & Kart, 1982). Noting this, Rowe and Kahn (1997) pinpointed engagement in leisure activities as one of the major prerequisites for successful ageing. Atchley (1989; see also 1998) later put forward a revision to this theory, moving the spotlight from the amount of activity to the *continuity* of lifestyle and the ability of older people to adapt to the constraints of ageing by substituting and redistributing activities. Continuity does not indeed necessarily mean the absence of any modification but may involve numerous adjustments: some activities that have become too demanding (physically or intellectually) are abandoned in favour of others, either in the same field or in a new one, that are more passive or more accessible (Bukov, Maas, & Lampert, 2002; Menec, 2003; Silverstein & Parker, 2002; Zimmer, Hickey, & Searle, 1997). Continuity of the lifestyle also means that a low level of activity does not necessarily imply a low level of well-being if the person's lifestyle is still in keeping with what it was before. This approach is close to that of theoretical models of a more psychological leaning which see in the ability to compensate for the erosion of physical and psychological capacities the key to successful ageing (e.g. Baltes, 1997; Baltes & Baltes, 1990; Brandtstädter & Rothermund, 2002; Staudinger, Freund, Linden, & Maas, 1999).

The analysis of links between leisure activities and well-being initially centred on retirement and the third age (see Palmore, 1979) but has since been extended to the fourth age, revealing that the pursuit of activities brings with it a whole series of positive effects, in particular a good level of well-being, whether this is measured in terms of life satisfaction, perceived quality of life, happiness, positive and negative affects (Herzog, Franks, Markus, & Holmberg, 1998; Menec, 2003; Menec & Chipperfield, 1997; Silverstein & Parker, 2002; Zimmer, Hickey, & Searle, 1995). The fact remains that, while there is solid evidence for the link between activity and well-being, less is known about the importance of keeping up the activity in very old age, a time when changes having a potentially negative impact on well-being take place, particularly changes connected with the deterioration of health. A certain amount of research shows that older people who continue their activities in the face of declining health conserve a good level of well-being (Atchley, 1998; Menec, 2003; Silverstein & Parker, 2002; Zimmer et al., 1995). But very few studies have focused on older people's ability to face the frailty process. Can they still maintain their activities and thus preserve their well-being face to the frailty process?

From a developmental viewpoint centred on changes throughout the life course, the frailty process designates the process peculiar to each individual of gradual and ineluctable degradation of the person's physiological and sensory-motor resources. Once a certain threshold (known in the literature as the threshold of insufficiency) has been reached, this process culminates in a state of *frailty*, which is typical of most of those who attain an advanced age. Frailty is considered to be multidimensional and to involve complex interactions between individual and environmental factors. It therefore corresponds more broadly to a *stage in the life course* in which functional dependence constitutes a limiting and in fact minority situation (for a literature review on the subject of frailty, see Spini, Ghisletta, Guilley, & Lalive d'Epinay, 2007). The onset and possible aggravation of frailty are thus crucial factors to be taken into account in analyzing the links between activity and well-being.

Frailty, in the form of serious impairment of an individual's physical or cognitive capacities or physical ailments of all sorts, may have a potentially harmful effect on that person's well-being. The challenge is then to determine the extent to which the continuity of activities is capable of counteracting this effect.

In activity theory, the idea of well-being is often reduced to that of life satisfaction. However, the scientific literature sees it as something more complex, generally distinguishing two dimensions partly independent of one another. The cognitive dimension refers to the subject's rating of his own life, either as a whole or in relation to certain specified fields (e.g. family, work and health). The perception of health, i.e. the self-assessment by the subject of his/her own health, is a good indicator of the cognitive dimension of well-being, bearing in mind that health is the major worry of the very old (Holahan, Holahan, & Wonacott, 2001). The affective dimension comprises all the individual's positive and negative affects (Diener & Suh, 1997; Hilleras, 1998). It is by no means certain that the nature or strength of the links between activity and well-being in advanced old age are the same for each dimension. Very little work has been done on this aspect but a study by Menec (2003), based on a longitudinal analysis, concluded that activity had a positive effect on the affective dimension but not on the cognitive dimension (life satisfaction).

Although there has been a surge in social science research focusing on advanced old age in recent years, there have so far been few longitudinal studies designed to monitor one or more cohorts of older persons over a lengthy time-span. Thus much remains to be done in order to describe and explain the processes that shape the existence of the elderly as they advance in years, particularly the many and complex ways in which biopsychological and social factors are intertwined. The longitudinal approach seems particularly suited to studying the relationship between activities and well-being. It provides a picture of the trajectories of activity as events unfold and health status evolves, and to identify their effects on well-being. Noteworthy among the rare longitudinal surveys that have been carried out are those of Silverstein and Parker (2002) and Menec (2003), which show that a reduction in the general level of activity triggers a slump in well-being.

Aims

This chapter deals with the consequences of frailty and of worsening frailty on both cognitive and affective dimensions of well-being of the very old. More specifically, using the data from Swilsoo (Swiss Interdisciplinary Longitudinal Study on the Oldest Old), it seeks to gauge the extent to which the continuity of leisure activities can counter the negative effects on well-being of frailty and its attendant repercussions.

METHODS

Participants

Only community-dwelling self-respondents who had followed at least one of the following health trajectories – either stable robustness or onset of frailty or stable frailty or aggravation of frailty (see procedure)- were taken into consideration (N=429 individuals, which totalled 1,329 questionnaires during the study period); interviews from institutionalized elderly were not taken into account in view of the nature of the information used (please, see chapter 1 for a description of the whole study).

Indicators

Well-being

We constructed two indicators, one per constituent of well-being. *Affective well-being* was measured using a modified version of the *Self-Assessing Depression Scale* (SADS, Wang, Treul, & Alverno, 1975) consisting of three positive affect items (having pleasure in doing things, having self-confidence, being hopeful about the future) and five negative items (feeling a little lonely, feeling sad, feeling anxious, finding time passes slowly, having crying spells or feeling like it), each being coded on a scale ranging from "never" to "always". The indicator thus constructed, after reversing the replies to the negative affect items, is the mean frequency of all eight items; a higher score therefore indicates a higher degree of affective well-being. *Cognitive well-being* is evaluated by means of a perception of health indicator resulting from the mean score obtained on two questions, one relating to the subjective assessment of health (self-rated health) and the other measuring the frequency of worries about health. These two questions were coded in an upward direction, so that a higher score indicates a more favourable perception of health. In view of the fact that for the second indicator the scales of the two items are different, and in order to make comparison of the two indicators possible, a process of standardisation at each wave on the basis of the first wave was applied in constructing the indicators (see Girardin Keciour & Spini, 2006).

Activities

The analysis is based on a list of 16 activities for which the interviewee had to say whether he/she had taken part in them over the past year and, if so, how often. The activities cover a wide range; some of them are carried out at home, others elsewhere; some require the presence of other people, others not. They fall into seven main categories: *manual activities* covering (1) gardening and (2) doing craftwork (knitting, fixing, mending, etc.); *games*, played either (3) alone (doing crossword, puzzles, etc) or (4) in company (cards, board games, chess, Scrabble, etc); the *media*, with (5) radio and (6) television; *reading*, either (7) a newspaper or (8) books or magazines; *outside activities* comprising (9) visiting coffees, tea rooms or restaurants, (10) attending local fairs or celebrations, (11) attending cultural events (theatre, music, cinema, etc.), (12) participating in trips or outings; *« physical » activities* consisting of (13) going for walks (besides shopping and going on errands) and (14) doing gymnastics or other physical exercises (besides walking); *religion* covering (15) praying and (16) attending religious services (which includes following such services on radio or television) (see Ghisletta, Bickel, & Lövden, 2006).

The various original scales were given a binary structure in order to distinguish between regular practice and little or no practice. The idea of regularity reflects the inclusion of the practice in the person's daily, weekly, monthly or annual routines, indicating that the practice in question forms part of the individual's lifestyle. Regularity obviously refers to different time scales for different activities. Reading a newspaper, for example, is part of the daily routine; going for walks and doing craftwork have a frequency of so many times a week; participating in trips or outings and attending local fairs or celebrations can be counted on an annual scale. In order to attribute a regular frequency threshold to each activity, we sought guidance from previous work (Bickel & Lalive d'Epinay, 2001; Bickel, Lalive d'Epinay, & Vollenwyder, 2005) and from an empirical examination of the frequency of the various activities. On that basis, we constructed an indicator summing the regular practices ranging from 0 to 16. This latter can show how lifestyle evolves in a situation of growing frailty, measured in terms of a stable or declining score for regular activities. The theoretical view of continuity that we have been following tells us that it is less the range of activities that is important than the way they evolve over time. In this context, our indicator provides a means of distinguishing between (a) continuity of lifestyle – which may cover forms of substitution between activities, depending on the person's ability to adapt, and (b) a change in lifestyle, which implies the cessation, or reduction below the regularity threshold, of one or more activities that are significant for the person in that they constitute a part of his/her lifestyle.

Frailty

Nineteen health disorders are grouped to represent five domains of health: mobility (going up and down stairs, moving around outside the home, walking at least 200 metres); physical pains (10 items; e.g. suffering a lot from pains in lower limbs), sensory capacities (reading a text in a newspaper, hearing in a conversation with another person, hearing in a conversation with several persons), memory (memory complaints), and energy (tiredness, loss of appetite). On this basis, three health statuses are defined: a person is ADL-dependent (D) if he/she is unable to perform alone one or more of the five activities of daily living (ADL, see Katz, Downs, Cash, & Grotz, 1970). A person reporting deficiencies in two or more health domains without incapacities in ADL was classified as ADL-independent frail (F) and the one with one or zero affected domains and no incapacities in ADL was considered as robust (R) (For more detail on the operationalisation of frailty, see Guilley, Armi, & Ghisletta, 2008a; Guilley et al., 2008b).

Other Variables

In this chapter we use six socio-demographic characteristics: age (in years); gender; socio-economic status (low versus medium/high); whether living alone; region (urban versus semi-rural); and cohort. Socio-economic status is a composite indicator combining socio-occupational category, level of education and income.

Procedure

Our study focuses on two health trajectories between two successive waves (*Wn* and *Wn+1*): firstly, the onset of ADL-independent frailty (R-F for short) and, secondly, the aggravation of ADL-independent frailty, seen as an increase in the number of health disorders (F-F+ for short). To simplify, ADL-independent frailty is named as frailty in the following text. We establish three profiles combining health trajectories with activity level. Profile I is made up of persons whose health status is stable (either stable robustness or stable frailty).

Profile II comprises individuals whose health declines (either the onset of frailty or the aggravation of frailty) and who maintain their level of activity. Profile III consists of persons whose health declines (either the onset of frailty or the aggravation of frailty) and who reduce their level of activity. Profile II and profile III are compared with profile I which is stable robustness in the case of the onset of frailty and stable frailty in the case of the aggravation of frailty.

The analysis is divided into three steps. First we evaluate how well-being and the proportion of regular participants in the 16 activities of our study evolve during the two frailty trajectories (the onset and the aggravation of frailty) using Wilcoxon and McNemar tests. The second step is to see how well-being evolves for each of the three profiles during the two frailty trajectories using Wilcoxon tests. In a third step, we compare the impact on well-being of the three profiles during the onset and the aggravation of frailty. In order to take into account other variables a multilevel analysis is carried out with well-being at wave *Wn+1* as the dependent variable and, as independent variables: (a) the three profiles, introduced in the form of two dummy variables, with profile I as reference category; (b) the level of well-being at wave *Wn*, so as to adjust the level of well-being under scrutiny in accordance with the situation at the beginning of the trajectory; and (c) the six socio-demographic variables mentioned above. While a comparison of the two cohorts reveals no differences in level of well-being, we add cohort as a control variable in the multivariate analysis in order to take into account possible variations in behaviour with time. It is worth noting that additional analysis testing for interactions between profiles and cohorts did not reveal any significant difference between cohorts. Other relational insertion variables measuring the frequency of contacts either with family members or with friends were tested but they are not included in the analyses because their effect is negligible and in no way alters the results presented. In contrast to Wilcoxon and McNemar tests, multilevel analyses provide a way of taking into account (and modelling) the fact that, in a design of that kind, the variability of observations is of dual origin, inter-individual and intra-individual. Furthermore they can tolerate an incomplete data set because they use all available data instead of restricting the analysis to individuals who participated to the nine waves of follow-up and therefore limit the selectivity effects (Raudenbush & Bryk, 2002; Snijders & Bosker, 1999).

RESULTS

Our sub-sample is composed of two cohorts, 47% of self-respondents belonging to the first one. Stratified by gender and region (urban versus semi-urban), it is made up of 49% of females and of 52% of city dwellers. Half of the subjects are of relatively low socio-economic status (50%). At their first interview considered here, most of them were cohabiting with one (usually the spouse) or more persons (55%). They were quite active since they were on average practicing regularly around nine activities. All the self-respondents were on average a satisfactory level of well-being, both affective and cognitive. Almost all of them reported having pleasure in doing things (98%), having self-confidence (95%) and being hopeful about the future (81%). Feeling anxious (14%), a little lonely (12%), sad (13%), finding time passes slowly (7%) and having crying spells or feeling like it (7%) were expressed by a minority.

More than half of them considered their state of health as good or very good (59%) and they rarely expressed concern for their health (12%).

Table 1 briefly presents the overall development of well-being and activities for persons who followed one or the other of the two trajectories of frailty. On the whole, both of them are associated with a decline in both cognitive and affective well-being. As for activities, in cases of both the onset and the aggravation of frailty, a fall-off in 4 of the 16 activities is noted, the fields concerned being mainly activities outside the home. In both health trajectories, the fall-off generates a sharp drop in the overall activity indicator.

Table 1. Levels of well-being and activity between two successive waves (Wn, Wn+1), by type of frailty trajectory

	Onset of frailty (R-F)			Aggravation of frailty (F-F+)		
	Wn	*Wn+1*	Sign	*Wn*	*Wn+1*	Sign
Well-being (mean scores)						
Affective well-being	0.19 (0.49)	0.11 (0.52)	**	-0.12 (0.61)	-0.23 (0.72)	**
Perception of health	0.25 (0.59)	0.06 (0.67)	***	-0.19 (0.79)	-0.40 (0.86)	**
Activities (% taking part)						
Watch television	90.6	87.6		92.6	92.7	
Listen to the radio	64.4	57.6	*	51.2	51.2	
Read the newspaper	84.9	85.7		84.7	86.1	
Read books and magazines	77.5	75.1		71.6	67.5	
Play games (cards, board games, chess, Scrabble)	32.7	29.3		31.4	29.8	
Do crossword puzzles	36.2	37.6		33.1	30.5	
Do gardening	29.7	25.2		25.8	20.1	*
Do craftwork (knit, fix, or mend)	40.1	35.4		34.7	31.1	
Go for walks (besides shopping and going on errands)	74.3	68.6	*	60.8	60.8	
Do gymnastics or other physical exercises (besides walking)	36.7	36.4		31.8	26.6	*
Visit coffees, tea rooms, restaurants	72.3	64.6	*	64.9	63.7	
Participate in trips or outings	54.1	45.5	*	48.8	42.6	
Attend cultural events (theater, music, cinema)	30.2	30.5		26.9	22.4	
Attend local fairs or celebrations	47.5	43.8		36.5	29.8	*
Pray	68.0	64.7		64.9	64.6	
Religious services (total) [1]	63.1	61.9		59.2	57.8	
(of whom : attend the service)	49.1	43.5		40.8	36.1	*
Average number of activities (0-16)	9.01 (2.38)	8.48 (2.49)	***	8.17 (2.41)	7.72 (2.54)	***

Wilcoxon tests (well-being and activity scores) and McNemar test (proportion of regular participants), *p<.05; **p<.01; ***p<.001.

[1] Including following the service on radio or television.

Onset of Frailty versus Stable Robustness

Table 2 shows that among cases of the onset of frailty, half of them are associated with continuity of activities (profile II) and the other half with a decrease in activities (profile III). What are the repercussions on well-being for each of the profiles? For profiles I and II, affective well-being remained stable; for profile III, in contrast, it deteriorated considerably. The picture for perception of health is somewhat different, a drop in well-being occurring not only for profile III but also for profile II.

Multilevel analyses confirm these results (table 3). Profile III shows a level of affective well-being much lower than profile I. On the other hand, the difference is statistically insignificant between profiles I and II. The level of cognitive well-being for profiles II and III is contrasting with that of profile I. When well-being at the start of the trajectory is taken into account, no control variable has any effect on perception of health. Affective well-being is however slightly lower among the city dwellers.

Table 2. Onset of frailty: well-being between two successive waves by profiles

		Affective well-being			Perception of health		
	%	*Wn*	*Wn+1*	Sign	*Wn*	*Wn+1*	Sign
Profile I	72	0.30	0.30		0.46	0.41	*
Profile II	13	0.17	0.18		0.21	0.06	*
Profile III	15	0.21	0.05	***	0.29	0.08	**

Wilcoxon tests: * p<.05; ** p<.01; *** p<.001.

Notes:

Profile I=stable robustness;

Profile II=onset of frailty with continuity of activities;

Profile III=onset of frailty with decrease in activities.

Table 3. Onset of frailty and well-being: multivariate analysis

	Regression coefficient β (standard errors)	
	Affective well-being	Perception of health
Profile II vs Profile I	-0.05 (0.04)	-0.24 (0.06)***
Profile III vs Profile I	-0.18 (0.04)***	-0.25 (0.06)***
Affective well-being at *Wn*	0.44 (0.07)***	
Perception of health at *Wn*		0.47 (0.04)***
Age	-0.00 (0.01)	0.01 (0.01)
Gender (female)	0.01 (0.04)	0.00 (0.05)
Socio-economic status (medium/high)	0.06 (0.04)	0.04 (0.04)
Region (urban)	-0.08 (0.04)*	-0.07 (0.04)
Cohort (first)	-0.06 (0.03)	0.02 (0.04)
Living alone (yes)	-0.08 (0.04)	-0.01 (0.05)

* p<.05; **p<.01; *** p<.001

Table 4. Aggravation of frailty: well-being between two successive waves by profiles

		Affective well-being			Perception of health		
	%	*Wn*	*Wn+1*	Sign	*Wn*	*Wn+1*	Sign
Profile I	54	-0.06	-0.06		-0.22	-0.11	**
Profile II	25	-0.19	-0.25		-0.21	-0.28	
Profile III	21	-0.03	-0.20	**	-0.11	-0.50	***

Wilcoxon tests: * p<.05; ** p<.01; *** p<.001.

Notes:

Profile I=stable frailty;

Profile II=aggravation of frailty with continuity of activities;

Profile III=aggravation of frailty with decrease in activities.

Aggravation of Frailty versus Stable Frailty

Table 4 shows that half of the cases refer to profile I (here stable frailty) and the other half is associated with the aggravation of frailty. These latter cases are more or less equally divided between profiles II (continuity of activity) and III (decrease in activities). The pattern of change in affective well-being is similar to that observed for the onset of frailty: a sharp drop for profile III and stability for profiles I and II. For perception of health, the picture is the same, with profile III plummeting, profile II remaining steady and profile I even gaining a little.

Multilevel analyses confirm that profile III contrasts with profile I in that its scores for both affective and cognitive well-being are much lower. Profiles I and II are statistically indistinguishable. If we take the level of well-being at the start of the trajectory into account, advancing age exerts an effect on the affective well-being and the cohort on the cognitive well-being, perception of health being somewhat better in the first cohort.

Table 5. Aggravated frailty and well-being: multivariate analysis

	Regression coefficient β (standard errors)	
	Affective well-being	Perception of health
Profile II vs Profile I	-0.09 (0.06)	-0.15 (0.08)
Profile III vs Profile I	-0.15 (0.06)*	-0.45 (0.08)***
Affective well-being at *Wn*	0.57 (0.05)***	
Perception of health at *Wn*		0.43 (0.06)***
Age	-0.02 (0.01)*	-0.00 (0.01)
Gender (female)	-0.08 (0.06)	0.06 (0.07)
Socio-economic status (medium/high)	0.04 (0.05)	0.08 (0.07)
Region (urban)	-0.03 (0.05)	-0.06 (0.07)
Cohort (first)	0.06 (0.05)	0.14 (0.07)*
Living alone (yes)	-0.10 (0.05)	-0.03 (0.07)

* p<.05; ** p<.01; *** p<.001

Discussion

Our aim in this chapter was to answer the following question: does continuity of activities counter the adverse effect of frailty on well-being? Using a longitudinal research design, we scrutinised two types of trajectory corresponding to the onset of frailty and the aggravation of frailty. We concluded that the answer to our initial question was broadly in the affirmative. Our results show that in three out of the four situations envisaged (two types of frailty trajectory x two constituents of well-being), the frailty process generally undermined well-being but that this negative effect was greatly mitigated if not completely neutralised when the level of activity was maintained. Cognitive well-being was however the exception to the rule, plunging steeply with the onset of frailty regardless of the activity level. Despite this last case, our findings largely corroborate the theoretical model of continuity formulated by Atchley (1989) and the empirical work validating it.

As stated above, the continuity of activities as we defined and measured it does not necessarily imply invariability but may be the net outcome of various forms of compensation and substitution, as a number of authors have pointed out (Bukov et al., 2002; Menec, 2003; Silverstein & Parker, 2002; Zimmer et al., 1997). In that sense, it can also be construed as an expression of frail people's adaptive capacity, in which one of the keys to successful ageing is to be found, according to various research papers and theoretical studies on self-regulation (e.g. Baltes, 1997; Baltes & Baltes, 1990; Brandtstädter & Rothermund, 2002; Staudinger, Freund, Linden, & Maas, 1999). Our findings are in line with those conclusions even though, in our work, we did not take into account the psychological mechanisms that constituted their centre of attention.

With regard to certain research work such as that of Menec (2003) which noted a difference in the impact of activity depending on the constituent of well-being concerned – cognitive or affective – our study gives mixed signals. While the onset of frailty prompts two different reactions, with the continuity of activity negating the fall in affective well-being but having no effect on perception of health, this contrast is absent in the case of worsening frailty, where the sustained rate of activity has a positive effect on both dimensions.

At the onset of frailty, loosing robustness might be perceived as a pronounced health decline by those who were so far in a healthy status. Therefore, the direct impact of the onset of frailty on perception of health may possibly be particularly strong, thus limiting the potential positive effect of activity. This latter result is in line with other studies showing the strong influence of objective health on the cognitive well-being (see Hoeymans, Feskens, Kromhout, & van den Bos, 1999; Pinquart, 2001; Rodin & McAvay, 1992). Much more research would be needed to clarify the similarities and differences in the way the constituents of well-being function in very old age.

As for the control variables, the level of affective well-being seems to be lower in the urban than in the semi-rural area (for the onset of frailty at least), a finding that is in conformity with those of rare studies asserting that elderly city dwellers are more prone to depression, anxiety and stress (Gale, 1993; Walters, Breeze, Wilkinson, Price, Bulpitt, & Fletcher, 2004). That said, little equivalent work seems to have been done, especially in Europe, covering all three aspects, well-being, health and the regional context in advanced old age. Further investigations are needed to examine more systematically the influence of context on well-being as the frailty process develops. Affective well-being also wanes with advancing age, at least in the case of worsening frailty. This finding, which is in line with Jang et al. (2004) but in contradiction to Adelmann (1994), suggests that, with time and with the growing weight of events or critical changes, the ability to adapt and to find new balances declines, sapping moral. However, none of these variables have any effect on perception of health. The latter, incidentally, is slightly more positive among members of the first cohort.

Neither gender nor socio-economic status affects well-being. While the absence of a gender effect runs counter to numerous research findings (Idler, 1993; Menec, 2003; Pinquart & Sörensen, 2001; Smith & Baltes, 1998), it is in keeping with other work (Menec & Chipperfield, 1997; Zimmer et al., 1995). The absence of a direct effect of socio-economic status on well-being seems surprising and is at variance with work done, for example, by Adelmann (1994), Jang et al. (2004), Kubzansky, Berkman and Seeman (2000), Idler (1993) and Zimmer et al. (1995). But this result, which corroborates that of Menec and Chipperfield (1997), is less surprising when seen in the light of the study carried out by Herzog et al. (1998) (see also George, 1992), who found that a higher socio-economic status (which the authors measured by level of education) has a positive effect on well-being (measured by a depression indicator), but only indirectly through its positive effect on the level of activity, the latter in turn directly boosting well-being. With our analysis procedure, it was not possible to identify any such indirect effect but we show elsewhere (Bickel & Cavalli, 2008), using the same basic data, that a higher socio-economic status engenders a higher level of activity, irrespective of health status.

In conclusion, decline in activity essentially concerns activities outside the home. Our findings can therefore be seen as indicating more precisely the negative effect on well-being of withdrawal into the home, loss of contact with the outside and existence in a shrunken life-world. One suggested extension of our work would be to examine possible variations in well-being according to the type of activity.

Another perspective for research is opened by the fact that, in our work, we analyzed the decline in activity in conjunction with deterioration in health status; thus the waning of activity was seen from the angle of a constraint imposed by the condition of frailty, the end-result being a drop in the level of well-being. However, research undertaken in the context of disengagement theory (Cumming & Henry, 1961; Johnson & Barer, 1992) showed that the cessation of activity may also be a deliberate choice by the individual, with positive repercussions on well-being. It would therefore be interesting to investigate how these two processes (i.e. constraint and voluntary disengagement) combine in a situation of frailty, whether they originate in differences of attitude between individuals and, if so, how these differences can be explained, to what extent they can succeed one another and, again if so, what are the factors that lead to one process or the other.

References

Adelmann, P. K. (1994). Multiple roles and psychological well-being in a national sample of older adults. *Journal of Gerontology, 49*(6), S277-S285.

Atchley, R. C. (1989). A continuity theory of normal aging. *The Gerontologist, 29*(2), 183-190.

Atchley, R. C. (1998). Activity adaptations to the development of functional limitations and results for subjective well-being in later adulthood: A qualitative analysis of longitudinal panel data over a 16-year period. *Journal of Aging Studies, 12*(1), 19-38.

Baltes, P. B. (1997). On the incomplete architecture of human ontogeny. Selection, optimization, and compensation as foundation of developmental theory. *American Psychologist, 52*(4), 366-380.

Baltes, P. B., & Baltes, M. M. (1990). Psychological perspectives on successful aging: A model of selective optimization with compensation. In P. B. Baltes, & M. M. Baltes (Eds.), *Successful aging: Perspectives from the behavioral sciences* (pp. 1-34). New York: Cambridge University Press.

Bickel, J.-F., & Cavalli, S. (2008). Activités de loisir et pratiques religieuses [social activities and religious practices]. In C. Lalive d'Epinay, & D. Spini (Eds.), *Les années fragiles. La vie au-delà de quatre-vingts ans* (pp. 247-280). Québec: Presses de l'Université de Laval.

Bickel, J.-F., & Lalive d'Epinay, C. (2001). Les styles de vie des personnes âgées et leur évolution récente: une étude de cohortes [Life styles of the elders and their recent trend: a cohort analysis]. In M. Legrand (Ed.), *La retraite: une révolution silencieuse* (pp. 245-280). Ramonville Saint-Agne: Erès.

Bickel, J.-F., Lalive d'Epinay, C., & Vollenwyder, N. (2005). Changement et continuité dans les loisirs: une comparaison de cohortes [Change and continuity in leisure activities: a comparison of cohorts] *L'Année Sociologique, 55*(1), 129-170.

Brandtstädter, J., & Rothermund, K. (2002). The life course dynamics of goal pursuit and goal adjustment: A two-process framework. *Developmental Review, 22*(1), 117-150.

Cumming, E., & Henry, W. H. (1961). *Growing old: The process of disengagement.* New York: Basic Books.

Diener, E., & Suh, M. E. (1997). Subjective well-being and age: An international analysis. *Annual Review of Gerontology and Geriatrics, 17*, 304-324.

Gale, B. J. (1993). Psychosocial health needs of older women: Urban versus rural comparisons. *Archives of Psychiatric Nursing, 7*(2), 99-105.

George, L. K. (1992). Economic status and subjective well-being: A review of the literature and an agenda for future research. In D. W. Gregg, N. E. Cutler, & M. P. Lawton (Eds.), *Aging, money, and life satisfaction: Aspects of financial gerontology* (pp. 69-99). New York: Springer Publishing Company.

Ghisletta, P., Bickel, J.-F., & Lövden, M. (2006). Does activity engagement protect against cognitive decline in old age? Methodological and analytical considerations. *Journal of Gerontology: Psychological Sciences, 61B*, P253-P261.

Girardin Keciour, M., & Spini, D. (2006). Well-being and frailty process in later life: An evaluation of the effectiveness of downward social comparison. *Swiss Journal of Sociology, 32*(3), 389-406.

Guilley, E., Armi, F., & Ghisletta, P. (2008a). Indépendance-fragilité-dépendance: trois statuts de santé [Robustness, frailty, ADL-dependence: Three health statuses]. In C. Lalive d'Epinay, & D. Spini (Eds.), *Les années fragiles. La vie au-delà de quatre-vingts ans* (pp. 101-122). Québec: Les Presses de l'Université de Laval.

Guilley, E., Ghisletta, P., Armi, F., Berchtold, A., Lalive d'Epinay, C., Michel, J.-P., et al. (2008b). Dynamics of frailty and ADL-dependence in a five-year longitudinal study of octogenarians. *Research on Aging, 30*(3), 299-317.

Havighurst, R. J., Neugarten, B. L., & Tobin, S. S. (1968). Disengagement and patterns of aging. In B. L. Neugarten (Ed.), *Middle age and aging. A reader in social psychology* (pp. 161-172). Chicago: The University of Chicago Press.

Herzog, R. A., Franks, M. M., Markus, H. R., & Holmberg, D. (1998). Activities and well-being in older age: effects of self-concept and educational attainment. *Psychology and Aging, 13*(2), 179-185.

Hilleras, P. (1998). *Well-being among the very old: A survey on a sample aged 90 years and above*. Stockholm: Karolinska Institute and Stockholm Gerontology Research Center.

Holahan, C. K., Holahan, C. J., & Wonacott, N. L. (2001). Psychological well-being at age 80: health-related and psychological factors. *Journal of Mental Health and Aging, 7*(4), 395-411.

Idler, E. L. (1993). Age differences in self-assessments of health: Age changes, cohort differences, or survivorship? *Journal of Gerontology, 48*(6), S289-S300.

Jang, Y., Mortimer, J. A., Haley, W. E., & Borenstein Graves, A. R. (2004). The role of social engagement in life satisfaction: Its significance among older individuals with disease and disability. *Journal of Applied Gerontology, 23*(3), 266-278.

Johnson, C. L., & Barer, B. M. (1992). Patterns of engagement and disengagement among the oldest old. *Journal of Aging Studies, 6*(4), 351-364.

Katz, S., Downs, T. D., Cash, H. R., & Grotz, R. C. (1970). Progress in development of the index of ADL. *The Gerontologist, 10*(1), 20-30.

Kubzansky, L. D., Berkman, L. F., & Seeman, T. E. (2000). Social conditions and distress in elderly persons: Findings from the MacArthur studies of successful aging. *Journal of Gerontology: Psychological Sciences, 55B*(4), P238-P246.

Lemon, B. W., Bengtson, V. L., & Peterson, J. A. (1972). An exploration of the activity theory of aging: Activity types and life satisfaction among in-movers to a retirement community. *Journal of Gerontology, 27*(4), 511-523.

Longino, C. F., & Kart, C. S. (1982). Explicating activity theory: A formal replication. *Journal of Gerontology, 37*(6), 713-722.

Menec, V. H. (2003). The relation between everyday activities and successful aging: A six-year longitudinal study. *Journal of Gerontology: Social Sciences, 58B*(2), S74-S82.

Menec, V. H., & Chipperfield, J. G. (1997). Remaining active in later life. The role of locus of control in seniors' leisure activity participation, health, and life satisfaction. *Journal of Aging and Health, 9*(1), 105-125.

Palmore, E. B. (1979). Predictors of successful aging. *The Gerontologist, 19*(5), 427-431.

Pinquart, M., & Sörensen, S. (2001). Gender differences in self-concept and psychological well-being in old age: A meta-analysis. *Journal of Gerontology: Psychological Sciences, 56B*(4), P195-P213.

Raudenbush, S. W., & Bryk, A. S. (2002). *Hierarchical linear models. Applications and data analysis methods* (2nd ed.). Thousand Oaks: Sage

Rowe, J. W., & Kahn, R. L. (1997). Successful aging. *The Gerontologist, 37*(4), 433-440.

Silverstein, M., & Parker, M. G. (2002). Leisure activities and quality of life among the oldest old in Sweden. *Research on Aging, 24*(5), 528-547.

Smith, J., & Baltes, M. M. (1998). The role of gender in very old age: Profiles of functioning and everyday life patterns. *Psychology and Aging, 13*(4), 676-695.

Snijders, T. A. B., & Bosker, R. J. (1999). *Multilevel analysis. An introduction to basic and advanced multilevel modeling*. London: Sage.

Spini, D., Ghisletta, P., Guilley, E., & Lalive d'Epinay, C. (2007). Frail elderly. In J. E. Birren (Ed.), *Encyclopedia of gerontology. Age, aging, and the aged* (2nd ed., Vol. 1, pp. 572-579). San Diego: Elsevier, Academic Press.

Staudinger, U. M., Freund, A. M., Linden, M., & Maas, I. (1999). Self, personality, and life regulation: Facets of psychological resilience in old age. In P. B. Baltes, & K. U. Mayer (Eds.), *The Berlin Aging Study: Aging from 70 to 100* (pp. 302-328). Cambridge, U.K.: Cambridge University Press.

Walters, K., Breeze, E., Wilkinson, P., Price, G. M., Bulpitt, C. J., & Fletcher, A. (2004). Local area deprivation and urban-rural differences in anxiety and depression among people older than 75 years in Britain. *American Journal of Public Health, 94*(10), 1768-1774.

Wang, R. I., Treul, S., & Alverno, L. (1975). A brief self-assessing depression scale. *Journal of Clinical Pharmacology, 15*(2-3), 163-167.

Zimmer, Z., Hickey, T., & Searle, M. S. (1995). Activity participation and well-being among older people with arthritis. *The Gerontologist, 35*(4), 463-471.

In: The Closing Chapters of Long Lives
Editors: E. Guilley, Ch. J. Lalive d'Epinay

ISBN: 978-1-60456-971-1

Chapter 10

THE PARADOX OF WELL-BEING IN LATER LIFE: EFFECTIVENESS OF DOWNWARD SOCIAL COMPARISON DURING THE FRAILTY PROCESS

Myriam Girardin, Dario Spini and Valérie-Anne Ryser*

ABSTRACT

This chapter, which is based on a ten-year longitudinal study conducted with two cohorts of octogenarians, examines downward social comparison as an adjustment mechanism and its impact on well-being during the frailty process. The cognitive and affective dimensions of well-being are both taken into consideration. Our population of analysis was made up of self-respondents, aged between 80 and 84 at baseline. Descriptive analyses and multilevel models were used to examine the links between well-being, downward social comparison and the frailty process. A paradoxically slow decline in well-being was first observed over the ten years notwithstanding the general decline in health. Further analysis showed that the decline in well-being with encroaching frailty was less marked in the case of those who applied downward social comparison than those who did not. These results demonstrate that downward social comparison is an effective adjustment mechanism even in a population which, because of its advanced age, is more and more afflicted by frailty.

INTRODUCTION

This chapter investigates the progress of well-being in very old age, focusing on an adjustment mechanism – downward social comparison – sometimes used by older people in order to cope with the challenges of advanced old age. Considered in a broad sense, very old

* Correspondence concerning this chapter should be addressed to Myriam Girardin, Center for Interdisciplinary Gerontology, Rte de Drize 7, Site Battelle, CH – 1227 Carouge, gmyriam1@yahoo.com

age is a time of frailty, defined as a gradual failing in various dimensions of health (biophysical, motor-sensory, cognitive, etc.), which may lead to loss of autonomy (Spini, Ghisletta, Guilley, & Lalive d'Epinay, 2007b). The question is: how does the well-being of the very old evolve in reaction to this process? In this chapter, we consider the two constituents of well-being as defined in the scientific literature, namely, the affective dimension, comprising the positive and negative affects of individuals, and the cognitive dimension, comprising self-evaluation of one's own life or of more specific subjects (family, health, etc.) (Diener, Suh, Lucas, & Smith, 1999; Diener & Suh, 1997; Hilleras, 1998). The perception of health, i.e. the self-assessment by the subject of his/her own health, may be a good indicator of the cognitive dimension, bearing in mind that health is the major worry of the very old (Holahan, Holahan, & Wonacott, 2001).

The Paradoxical Stability of Well-being with Age

A number of researchers relate the decline in the affective dimension of well-being to advancing age but are astonished by the slow rate of that decline, considering the deterioration in health which is typical of the ageing process (Fiske, Gatz, & Pedersen, 2003; Jopp & Rott, 2006; Rothermund & Brandtstädter, 2003). The same can be said of the cognitive dimension; objective and subjective health are both measures of the same reality but are not systematically correlated. More surprisingly, the correlation between the two weakens further with advancing age to a point where, on average, the perception of health detaches itself entirely from the declining trend in objective health (Hoeymans, Feskens, Kromhout, & van den Bos, 1999; Idler, 1993; Leinonen, Heikkinen, & Jylhä, 2001; Pinquart, 2001; Rodin & McAvay, 1992). The divergent directions taken by well-being, which tends to decline slowly, and health, which tends to decline more steeply, are perceived as a paradox (Jopp & Rott, 2006; Kunzmann, Little, & Smith, 2000).

An Effective Adjustment Mechanism: Downward Social Comparison

This paradox is explained in the literature by the observation that older people call into play certain mechanisms which enable them to adapt to declining health, thus helping to preserve their well-being (Brandtstädter & Greve, 1994; Heckhausen & Schulz, 1995; Holahan et al., 2001; Idler, 1993; Kunzmann et al., 2000; Rothermund & Brandtstädter, 2003). Of these mechanisms, downward social comparison seems particularly effective in old age and is so frequently used as to be a constant feature of elders' statements when they are rating their own state of health (Henchoz, Cavalli, & Girardin, 2008). It involves comparing oneself with similar others (e. g. contemporaries or people suffering from the same illness) who are worse off or less fortunate (Wood, 1989). It enables individuals who feel relatively advantaged to preserve or to enhance their self-esteem (Frieswijk, Buunk, Steverink, & Slaets, 2004; Heckhausen & Schulz, 1995; Spini, Clémence, & Ghisletta, 2007a; Suls, Marco, & Tobin, 1991; Taylor, 1983; Taylor & Lobel, 1989; Wood, 1989). Thus, by evaluating themselves in comparison with others who are in poorer health, older people can minimize the impairments to their own health, which they then consider normal to such a degree that some impairments – even of a disabling nature – have less influence on their well-being (Brandtstädter & Greve, 1994; Leinonen, Heikkinen, & Jylhä, 2001).

Aim

The chief aim of this chapter is to assess the effectiveness of downward social comparison as an adjustment mechanism in the course of the frailty process. We do this by proceeding in two stages. To start with, we check the veracity of the paradox of well-being against our own data. Most of the above-mentioned studies describing this paradox relate to a younger population than ours or are based on cross-sectional data (e.g. Jopp & Rott, 2006). Knowing that our population is of an advanced age and is therefore well engaged in the frailty process (Guilley et al., 2008), we seek confirmation that the same phenomenon applies.

We follow up this first stage by looking more specifically at downward social comparison and its beneficial effect on well-being during the frailty process. Previous research highlighted the regulatory role played by downward social comparison in confronting health problems but most of the studies in question were founded essentially on cross-sectional data (Frieswijk et al., 2004; Holahan et al., 2001; Suls et al., 1991) or, if they were longitudinal, considered health decline either from the standpoint of one dimension only (e.g. functional health) or from that of several dimensions but tested separately (Leinonen et al., 2001; Spini et al., 2007a). The multidimensional nature of the frailty process was thus often disregarded. That being so, the longitudinal data available from the Swilsoo (Swiss Interdisciplinary Longitudinal Study on the Oldest Old) survey provide a useful opportunity to assess over a long period - ten years - the effectiveness of downward social comparison in maintaining the well-being of a population which, because of its advanced age, was becoming increasingly frail.

METHODS

Participants

In view of the type of information we needed, we retained only self-respondent participants (N=652 at baseline, which totalled 2,496 interviews over the ten-year period). The selected self-respondent participants were in better health than the proxy respondents (please, see chapter 1 for a description of the study).

Measures

Well-being

Our analysis is based on nine questions designed to measure the frequency of positive and negative affects, using a scale ranging from "never" to "always" (scale adapted from the Wang Self-Assessing Depression Scale (SADS) cf. Wang, Treul, & Alverno, 1975). In addition, self-rated health, assessed by asking "Overall, how do you evaluate your health?", is taken into account, measured on a scale ranging from "poor" to "very good". Table 1 shows all these items and their frequency. The following two indicators were constructed on the basis of a principal component analysis on these ten items (standardized at each wave on the basis of the first wave) and by referring to the theoretical definition of well-being (Girardin Keciour & Spini, 2006):

(a) *Affective well-being*: this first indicator measures the mean frequency of all the positive affects (having pleasure in doing things, having self-confidence, being hopeful about the future) and the negative affects (feeling a little lonely, feeling sad, feeling anxious, finding that time passes slowly, having crying spells or feeling like it). The negative affect scales are inverted in order to obtain an overall positive indicator. Thus, a high score indicates that the persons interviewed considered on average that their affective well-being was very positive. This indicator measures the affective component of well-being.
(b) *Perception of health*: this indicator is the mean of two items, self-rated health and the frequency of the individual's concern for his/her own health. These two questions are positively coded; thus the higher the score, the more positive the perception of health. This indicator evaluates the cognitive component of well-being.

Frailty Process

An indicator of the number of health domain deficiencies was constructed using self-reported deficiencies in five health domains: mobility (going up and down stairs, moving around outside the home, walking at least 200 metres), physical pains (10 items, e.g. suffering a lot from pains in the lower limbs), sensory capacities (reading a text in a newspaper, hearing in a conversation with another person, hearing in a conversation with several persons), memory (memory complaints), and energy (tiredness, loss of appetite). Its scale ranges from 0 (no deficiency) to 5 (deficiencies in five domains of health). A person is deemed frail if he/she is impaired in at least two of these five dimensions. With two domains affected, frailty in very old persons indicates an increased risk of adverse outcomes, including dependence in the activities of daily living (ADL) and mortality (for a detailed description of frailty, see Guilley et al., 2008)

Social Comparison

To measure social comparison, we asked octogenarians to compare their own state of health with that of other persons of the same age. They could estimate that their state of health was worse, equivalent or better.

Socio-demographic Characteristics

In the present study we used five socio-demographic variables: age (in years), gender, socio-economic status (low versus medium/high), geographical area of residence (semi-rural versus urban) and cohort. Socio-economic status was measured taking into account the last occupational activity, level of education and income.

Plan of Analysis

This study seeks to clarify the relationship between well-being, health and downward social comparison in later life. The analysis consisted of three parts.

First, we described the evolution of health and well-being (mean scores) as a function of the age of the participants. We used as an indicator of health the inverted standardized (with respect to the first wave) indicator of the number of deficiencies in health domains. Well-being was considered in both its dimensions and was measured throughout by the two indicators, affective well-being and perception of health. Multilevel analyses were used to assess the relationship between health or well-being on the one hand, and the age of participants on the other. The regression coefficients indicate whether health or well-being increases ($\beta > 0$), decreases ($\beta < 0$) or stays the same (β not significantly different from zero) according to the age of participants. Multilevel analyses can tolerate an incomplete data set because they use all available data instead of restricting the scope to individuals who participated in all nine waves of the follow-up, thus limiting the selectivity effects.

Secondly, in order to assess the effect of downward social comparison on well-being as the frailty process evolved, we sought to determine graphically whether people using downward social comparison as an adjustment mechanism exhibited a better level of well-being and/or a slower decline in well-being, as the number of deficiencies in health domains increased.

Finally, multilevel analysis was carried out to assess statistically the previous descriptive observations. We evaluated the relationship between well-being, as dependent variable, and, as independent variables: (a) the number of deficiencies in health domains; (b) the downward social comparison; (c) the interaction between the number of deficiencies in health domains and the downward social comparison; and (d) the socio-demographic variables. Social comparison answers were divided in two categories: "better" and "equivalent or worse". The category "better" refers to the mechanism of downward social comparison. Age, the number of deficiencies in health domains, the downward social comparison and their interaction, assessed at each wave, were included as level-1, time-varying predictors, and gender, socio-economic status, geographic area and cohort as level-2, time-invariant predictors. Multilevel models were fitted by the method of restricted maximum likelihood and results were reported with a robust estimation of the standard errors. Multilevel analyses were conducted with HLM (Raudenbush, Bryk, Cheong, & Congdon, 2004).

Results

Well-being and Health at Baseline

Our initial sample was made up of self-respondents from both cohorts, the first (45%) and the second (55%). Stratified by gender and region, it contained as many women as men and as many representatives of the urban region as of the semi-rural region. The average age of the sample was 81.8 years (SD=1.39) at baseline and about half (52%) of the respondents were of low socio-economic status.

Most of the subjects who replied personally at the first interview (baseline) had a satisfactory level of well-being, both affective and cognitive (see Table 1). Almost all stated that they had pleasure in doing things (96%), that they were self-confident (92%), and that they were hopeful about the future (78%). The negative affects most often quoted were anxiety (16%), loneliness (14%), sadness (11%) and boredom (10%) but these referred to a minority. With regard to the cognitive dimension of well-being, over half of the elders (57%) deemed their health good or very good while the other half deemed it poor to satisfactory. But this did not prevent a majority from claiming that they seldom or never worried about their health (85%) or that they considered their health better than that of their peers (61%), even though, at the outset of the study, over half of them (55%) had at least two deficiencies in health domains.

Table 1. Well-being and health at baseline (N=652)

	%
Affective well-being[1]	
I have pleasure in doing things	96
I have self-confidence	92
I am hopeful about the future	78
I feel anxious	16
I feel a little lonely	14
I feel sad	11
I find time passes slowly	10
I have crying spells or feel like it	7
Perception of health	
I consider my state of health good to very good	57
I am worried about my health [1]	15
Social comparison	
My health is better than that of my peers	61
My health is equivalent to that of my peers	33
My health is worse than that of my peers	6
Persons having 2 to 5 deficiencies in health domains	55

[1] Percentage of those stating that they feel these affects often to always.

Evolution of Well-being and Health with Age

Figure 1 shows the average scores of the two dimensions of well-being and of health – measured by the inverted standardized indicator of the number of deficiencies in health domains - as a function of the age of participants. It is clear that health declines markedly with advancing age. Its standardized average score goes from 0.07 at the age of 80 to -0.49 at age 90 and over (β = -0.07, p <.001), which is equivalent to a rise from 1.8 to 2.6 in the average number of deficiencies in health domains. This deterioration is reflected in the falling proportion of healthy subjects (having less than two deficiencies in health domains), who made up 48% of the sample at age 80 but only 29% at 90 and over, while the proportion of persons having at least two deficiencies in health domains surged from 52% to 71%. The affective well-being (β=-0.02, p <.001) and the perception of health (β=-0.02, p =.007) also declined sharply with age. However, the decline in health was more than three times that in well-being (cf. β). Thus, our data confirm the paradoxically slow decline in well-being which has been identified in a number of studies.

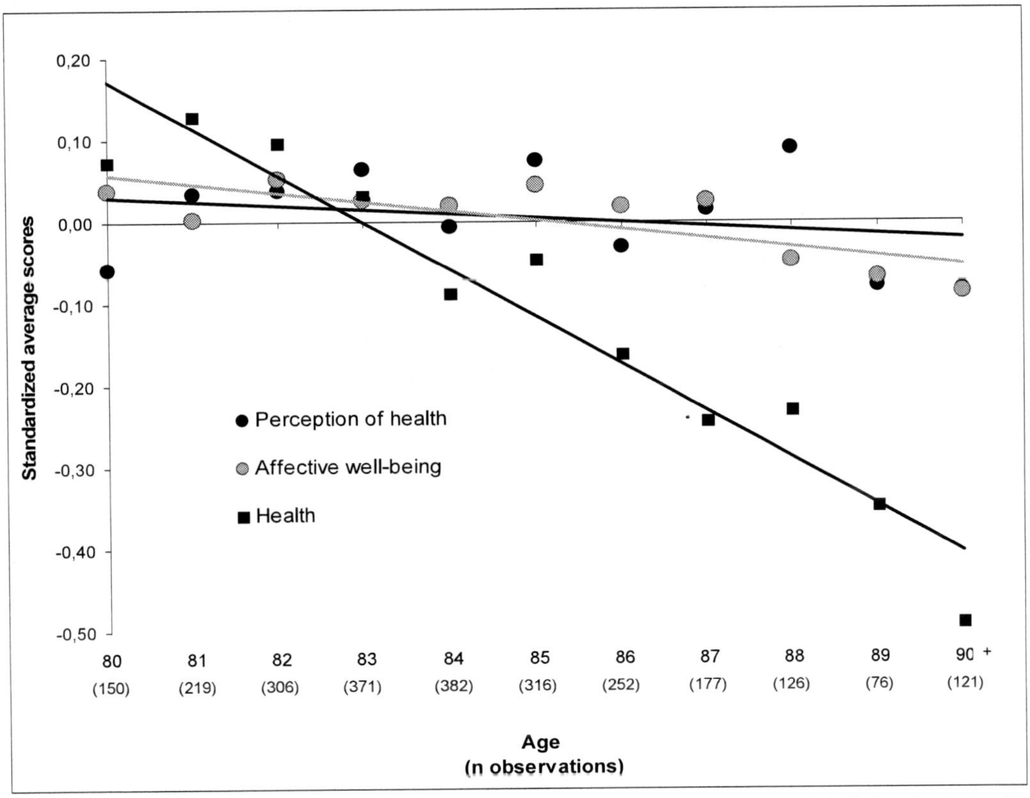

Note: The health indicator is the inverted standardized indicator of the number of deficiencies in health domains.

Figure 1. Standardized average scores of the two dimensions of well-being and of health, by age of respondents.

The Effectiveness of Downward Social Comparison during the Frailty Process

The diverging paths of well-being and health may possibly be explained by the beneficial effect of downward social comparison on well-being. In order to test this, we plotted the aggregate change in the two constituents of well-being by social comparison and the number of deficiencies in health domains (figure 2).

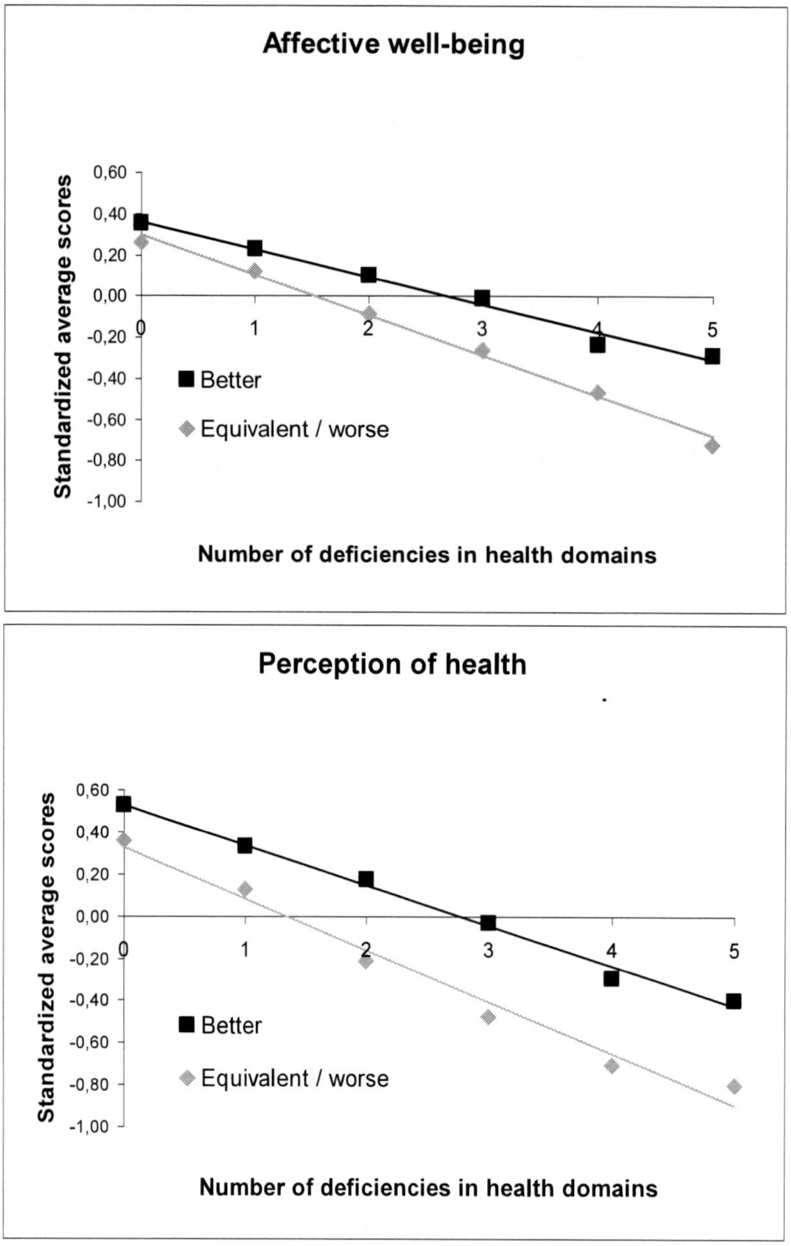

Figure 2. The two dimensions of well-being, by social comparison and number of deficiencies in health domains.

The two constituents of well-being both decline as the number of deficiencies in health domains increases. If social comparison is taken into account, however, the positive assessment of health (better) tends to go together with a higher level of well-being, both affective and cognitive, whatever the number of deficiencies in health domains. The graphs also show that the difference of level of well-being between the two groups (better and equivalent/worse) tends to increase as health deteriorates. The following analysis (table 2) will show whether or not this graphical trend can be confirmed.

Table 2. Multilevel analysis of affective well-being and perception of health

	Regression coefficient (standard errors)	
	Affective well-being [1]	**Perception of health [2]**
Gender (female)	-0.12 (0.04)**	0.08 (0.04)
Socio-economic status (middle/upper)	0.11 (0.04)**	0.08 (0.04)
Region (urban)	-0.10 (0.04)**	-0.03 (0.04)
Cohort (first)	0.00 (0.04)	0.04 (0.04)
Age (years)	-0.01 (0.01)*	-0.00 (0.01)
Number of deficiencies in health domains	-0.14 (0.02)***	-0.21 (0.02)***
Downward social comparison (better)	0.04 (0.04)	0.15 (0.05)**
Downward social comparison x number of deficiencies in health domains	0.05 (0.02)**	0.06 (0.02)**

Note: Number of observations for affective well-being: N=2,288; for perception of health: N=2,291.

[1] The higher the coefficient, the higher the affective well-being.

[2] The higher the coefficient, the more positive the perception of health.

* p<.05; ** p<.01; *** p<.001.

This analysis shows that deteriorating health has a distinct negative effect on both cognitive and affective well-being: the greater the number of deficiencies in health domains the lower the score for each constituent of well-being. It also shows that, among persons having the same health status, those who used downward social comparison enjoyed at the outset a better level of well-being than the others, but only in cognitive well-being. There was no difference in affective well-being. With growing frailty, however, a difference appears. The strong interaction between downward social comparison and number of deficiencies in health domains indicates that persons who consider their health better than that of their peers exhibit a decline in well-being, both affective and cognitive, that is less marked (the slope is less steep) than in the case of individuals who consider their health status the same or poorer. Downward social comparison thus seems to attenuate the decline in affective and cognitive well-being as frailty worsens. Whereas perception of health is impervious to other factors, affective well-being not only declines with age but is also lower among women, persons of low socio-economic status, and city dwellers.

Discussion

The objective of this study was (a) to check against our own data the veracity of the paradox of well-being, and (b) to assess the effectiveness of downward social comparison as an adjustment mechanism during the frailty process.

The well-being of our population of analysis declined only slowly over the ten-year period despite an obvious decline in health. The paradox of well-being (Kunzmann et al., 2000), noted in numerous studies (Fiske, Gatz, & Pedersen, 2003; Hoeymans, Feskens, Kromhout, & van den Bos, 1999; Idler, 1993; Jopp & Rott, 2006; Leinonen et al., 2001;

Pinquart, 2001; Rodin & McAvay, 1992; Rothermund & Brandtstädter, 2003), is corroborated by our own data, even though our population was an older one than that of most previous studies and was therefore subject to many health problems triggered by the frailty process. This bears out the conclusion of numerous studies (Baltes & Baltes, 1990; Brandtstädter & Greve, 1994; Carstensen, 1991; Heckhausen & Schulz, 1995), that the very old, despite their declining health, are always able to mobilise effective means of adjustment in order to cope with the inevitable frailty process. Among the various possible methods of adjustment, we chose to investigate the regulatory role of downward social comparison, the effectiveness of which in dealing with serious health problems has been widely described in the literature, including both cross-sectional studies (Brandtstädter & Greve, 1994; Frieswijk et al., 2004; Heckhausen & Schulz, 1995; Taylor, 1983; Taylor & Lobel, 1989) and longitudinal studies (Leinonen et al., 2001; Spini et al., 2007a). However it is worth noting that ours is one of the very few longitudinal studies that examine downward social comparison as an adjustment mechanism during the frailty process.

Our findings confirm the functional nature of this mechanism of adjustment: for persons having the same objective health status, the better the assessment of health compared with others of the same age, the higher the level of affective and cognitive well-being. Even among the very frail, those who apply this mechanism show a better level of well-being than those who do not, which is consistent with the findings of Frieswijk and co-workers (Frieswijk et al., 2004). That said, however, our results also show the adverse effect of failing health on well-being: on average, the two dimensions of well-being both decline as the number of deficiencies in health domains mounts. But – and here lies the originality of our research – this decline is much slower when downward social comparison is applied. Our analyses clearly reveal that, the greater the number of deficiencies in health domains, the wider the disparity between those who apply this mechanism and those who do not. In other words, downward social comparison seems to retard the decline in well-being during the frailty process, even in a very old population. Thus, by envisaging their health condition in a positive manner – even if, objectively speaking, their state of health is not as good – very old people are able to preserve their self-esteem, and therefore their well-being, as frailty worsens.

Certain socio-demographic variables also have a bearing on well-being, but only on its affective constituent. For example – levels of health status being equal – age is correlated with a sharp drop in affective well-being. It would seem that the capacity of the very old to adjust wanes with the gradual shrinking of resources that accompanies advancing age (Rothermund & Brandtstädter, 2003). Coping effectively with negative events – whether or not health-related (the loss of a loved one, for example) – thus becomes increasingly difficult with time (see Clémence, Karmaniola, Green, & Spini, 2007). Affective well-being also depends on gender: for a given state of objective health, women exhibit a lower level of affective well-being than men. This phenomenon has been widely reported in the literature, where it is explained by women's greater affective involvement in family matters and, as frequently happens, the need to look after an elderly, ailing husband, but also by their lower level of education (Antonucci, 2001; George, 1992b; Pinquart & Sörensen, 2001; Smith & Baltes, 1998). As other studies have shown, affective well-being is also linked to socio-economic status: for a given state of objective health, persons of higher socio-economic status have a better level of affective well-being than those of low status (George, 1992; Herzog, Franks, Markus, & Holmberg, 1998; Kubzansky, Berkman, & Seeman, 2000; Wrosch,

Heckhausen, & Lachman, 2000). Here, the explanatory factors proffered include the ability to keep up a life style (including leisure activities) more easily and the greater capacity to adjust (more effective coping strategies) of socially advantaged elders. Lastly, for a given state of health, the level of affective well-being is lower among city dwellers, a finding in line with studies that have shown the greater susceptibility of older city dwellers to stress, anxiety and depression (Gale, 1993; Walters, Breeze, Wilkinson, Price, Bulpitt, & Fletcher, 2004). According to our research, there is no link between perception of health, the cognitive dimension of well-being, and any of these socio-demographic variables. It would seem therefore that affective well-being is more sensitive to the life situation of the very old (e.g. women's family responsibilities, socio-economic situation, environment) than perception of health.

Our study's major strength lies in the actual design of the Swilsoo survey, which monitored over a period of ten years a population consisting initially of 652 octogenarians (self-respondents). Moreover, persons who moved into an institution during the period kept their place in our sample. As a result, our population of analysis was a very diverse one, from the point of view of life situation as well as health. The large size of the sample, the duration of the observations and the diversity of the population all helped to confer a substantial degree of robustness on our results.

None the less, the way our population of analysis was selected can be seen as a limiting factor. Only those persons who could answer our questions personally were retained. Clearly, such a restriction was necessitated by the subject of the chapter itself: proxies are scarcely in a position to make any pronouncements on the affective well-being or the perception of health of the person they speak for. Be that as it may, the well-being of proxy respondents is a matter deserving attention. Despite their poorer health, are they still able to apply downward social comparison or other adjustment mechanisms? And if so, do they apply them in a functional manner? In any case, the heterogeneity of our population of analysis as regards health is ensured by the fact that our analysis covered institutionalised self-respondents as well as individuals suffering from numerous health disorders.

Another limitation of our work was our inclusion of self-reported measures of frailty. The overestimation of health status – an outcome of downward social comparison – obviously influences also the replies of the very old to questions about their health problems. This is all the more likely when the health dimensions concerned are not clearly observable phenomena, e.g. memory or energy. How could this kind of influence affect our results? Very old persons who consider their state of health to be better than that of others may in fact suffer from deficiencies in more health domains than they assert. Their level of well-being would therefore be correspondingly more positive if the real number of deficiencies was taken into account, i.e. if the deficiencies had been measured in a more objective manner. Consequently, recognition of this bias does not invalidate our results. On the contrary, it reinforces them because the difference in well-being between those who apply downward social comparison and those who do not would be even greater if the real number of deficiencies was taken into account.

In this chapter, we chose to take an overall view of the relationship between downward social comparison, well-being and the process of frailty. An interesting perspective for research would be to analyse individual health trajectories, which would provide a representative sample of the various health situations prevailing in advanced old age. By analyzing these trajectories, a better assessment of the effectiveness of social comparison in a range of health contexts could be obtained. In particular, its effectiveness in a context of rapid health change such as the onset of chronic dependence could be gauged.

REFERENCES

Baltes, P. B., & Baltes, M. M. (1990). Psychological perspectives on successful aging: A model of selective optimization with compensation. In P. B. Baltes, & M. M. Baltes (Eds.), *Successful aging: Perspectives from the behavioral sciences* (pp. 1-34). New York: Cambridge University Press.

Brandtstädter, J., & Greve, W. (1994). The aging self: Stabilizing and protective processes. *Developmental Review, 14*(1), 52-80.

Carstensen, L. L. (1991). Selectivity theory: Social activity in life-span context. *Annual Review of Gerontology and Geriatrics, 11*, 195-217.

Clémence, A., Karmaniola, A., Green, E. G., & Spini, D. (2007). Disturbing life events and wellbeing after 80 years of age: A longitudinal comparison of survivors and the deceased over five years. *Ageing and Society, 27*(1), 1-19.

Diener, E., Suh, E. M., Lucas, R. E., & Smith, H. L. (1999). Subjective well-being: three decades of progress. *Psychological Bulletin, 125*(2), 276-302.

Diener, E., & Suh, M. E. (1997). Subjective well-being and age: An international analysis. *Annual Review of Gerontology and Geriatrics, 17*, 304-324.

Fiske, A., Gatz, M., & Pedersen, N. L. (2003). Depressive symptoms and aging: The effects of illness and non-health-related events. *Journal of Gerontology: Psychological Sciences, 58B*(6), P320-P328.

Frieswijk, N., Buunk, B. P., Steverink, N., & Slaets, J. P. J. (2004). The interpretation of social comparison and its relation to life satisfaction among elderly people: Does frailty make a difference? *Journal of Gerontology: Psychological Sciences, 59B*(5), P250-P257.

Gale, B. J. (1993). Psychosocial health needs of older women: Urban versus rural comparisons. *Archives of Psychiatric Nursing, 7*(2), 99-105.

George, L. K. (1992). Economic status and subjective well-being: A review of the literature and an agenda for future research. In D. W. Gregg, N. E. Cutler, & M. P. Lawton (Eds.), *Aging, money, and life satisfaction: Aspects of financial gerontology* (pp. 69-99). New York: Springer Publishing Company.

Girardin Keciour, M., & Spini, D. (2006). Well-being and frailty process in later life: An evaluation of the effectiveness of downward social comparison. *Swiss Journal of Sociology, 32*(3), 389-406.

Guilley, E., Ghisletta, P., Armi, F., Berchtold, A., Lalive d'Epinay, C., Michel, J.-P., et al. (2008). Dynamics of frailty and ADL-dependence in a five-year longitudinal study of octogenarians. *Research on Aging, 30*(3), 299-317.

Heckhausen, J., & Schulz, R. (1995). A life-span theory of control. *Psychological Review, 102*(2), 284-304.

Henchoz, K., Cavalli, S., & Girardin, M. (2008). Health perception and health status in advanced old age: A paradox of association. *Journal of Aging Studies, 22*(3).

Herzog, A. R., Franks, M. M., Markus, H. R., & Holmberg, D. (1998). Activities and well-being in older age: Effects of self-concept and educational attainment. *Psychology and Aging, 13*(2), 179-185.

Hilleras, P. (1998). *Well-being among the very old: A survey on a sample aged 90 years and above.* Stockholm: Karolinska Institute and Stockholm Gerontology Research Center.

Hoeymans, N., Feskens, E. J. M., Kromhout, D., & van den Bos, G. A. M. (1999). The contribution of chronic conditions and disabilities to poor self-rated health in elderly men. *Journal of Gerontology: Medical Sciences, 54A*(10), M501-M506.

Holahan, C. K., Holahan, C. J., & Wonacott, N. L. (2001). Psychological well-being at age 80: Health-related and psychological factors. *Journal of Mental Health and Aging, 7*(4), 395-411.

Idler, E. L. (1993). Age differences in self-assessments of health: Age changes, cohort differences, or survivorship? *Journal of Gerontology, 48*(6), S289-S300.

Jopp, D., & Rott, C. (2006). Adaptation in very old age: Exploring the role of resources, beliefs, and attitudes for centenarians' happiness. *Psychology and Aging 21*(2), 266-280.

Kubzansky, L. D., Berkman, L. F., & Seeman, T. E. (2000). Social conditions and distress in elderly persons: Findings from the MacArthur studies of successful aging. *Journal of Gerontology: Psychological Sciences, 55B*(4), P238-P246.

Kunzmann, U., Little, T. D., & Smith, J. (2000). Is age-related stability of subjective well-being a paradox? Cross-sectional and longitudinal evidence from the Berlin Aging Study. *Psychology and Aging, 15*(3), 511-526.

Leinonen, R., Heikkinen, E., & Jylhä, M. (2001). Predictors of decline in self-assessments of health among older people - a five-year longitudinal study. *Social Science and Medicine, 52*, 1329-1341.

Pinquart, M. (2001). Correlates of subjective health in older adults: A meta-analysis. *Psychology and Aging, 16*(3), 414-426.

Raudenbush, S. W., Bryk, A. S., Cheong, Y. F., & Congdon, R. T., Jr. (2004). *HLM 6: Hierarchical Linear and Nonlinear Modelling* (6th ed.). Lincolnwood, IL: Scientific Software International.

Rodin, J., & McAvay, G. J. (1992). Determinants of change in perceived health in a longitudinal study of older adults. *Journal of Gerontology: Psychological Sciences, 47*(6), P373-P384.

Rothermund, K., & Brandtstädter, J. (2003). Depression in later life: Cross-sequential patterns and possible determinants. *Psychology and Aging, 18*(1), 80-90.

Spini, D., Clémence, A., & Ghisletta, P. (2007a). How are temporal and social comparisons related to appraisals of self-rated health during very old age? *Swiss Journal of Psychology, 66*(2), 79-89.

Spini, D., Ghisletta, P., Guilley, E., & Lalive d'Epinay, C. (2007b). Frail elderly. In J. E. Birren (Ed.), *Encyclopedia of Gerontology. Age, aging, and the aged* (2nd ed., Vol. 1, pp. 572-579). San Diego: Elsevier, Academic Press.

Suls, J., Marco, C. A., & Tobin, S. (1991). The role of temporal comparison, social comparison, and direct appraisal in the elderly's self-evaluations of health. *Journal of Applied Social Psychology, 21*(14), 1125-1144.

Taylor, S. E. (1983). Adjustment to threatening events: A theory of cognitive adaptation. *American Psychologist, 38*(11), 1161-1173.

Taylor, S. E., & Lobel, M. (1989). Social comparison activity under threat: Downward evaluation and upward contacts. *Psychological Review, 96*(4), 569-575.

Walters, K., Breeze, E., Wilkinson, P., Price, G. M., Bulpitt, C. J., & Fletcher, A. (2004). Local area deprivation and urban-rural differences in anxiety and depression among people older than 75 years in Britain. *American Journal of Public Health, 94*(10), 1768-1774.

Wang, R. I., Treul, S., & Alverno, L. (1975). A brief self-assessing depression scale. *The Journal of Clinical Pharmacology, 15*(2-3), 163-167.

Wood, J. V. (1989). Theory and research concerning social comparisons of personal attributes. *Psychological Bulletin, 106*(2), 231-248.

Wrosch, C., Heckhausen, J., & Lachman, M. E. (2000). Primary and secondary control strategies for managing health and financial stress across adulthood. *Psychology and Aging, 15*(3), 387-399.

About the Authors

Franca Armi (M.A., sociologist), research assistant, CIG. (armif@bluewin.ch)

André Berchtold (Ph.D., statistician), senior lecturer and researcher at the Institute of Applied Mathematics, Faculty of Social and Political Sciences, University of Lausanne. (Andre.Berchtold@unil.ch)

Jean-François Bickel (Ph.D., sociologist), researcher at the CIG from 1992 to 2006. Since 2006, lecturer at the Department of social work and social politics, University of Fribourg. (Jean-Francois.Bickel@unifr.ch)

Stefano Cavalli (Ph.D., sociologist), assistant research professor at the CIG. (Stefano.Cavalli@cig.unige.ch)

Paolo Ghisletta (Ph.D., psychologist), research assistant professor (2001-2006), CIG. Since 2007, associate professor, Faculty of Psychology and Educational Sciences, University of Geneva. (Paolo.Ghisletta@pse.unige.ch)

Myriam Girardin (M.A., sociologist), research assistant, CIG. (gmyriam1@yahoo.com)

Luc Guillet (M.A., sociologist), research assistant, CIG, in charge of the Swilsoo database. (Luc.Guillet@cig.unige.ch)

Edith Guilley (Ph.D., natural scientist), methodologist. Assistant research professor at the CIG since 2001. Associate director of Swilsoo 2003-2008. (edith.guilley@orange.fr)

Christian J. Lalive d'Epinay (Ph. D., Dr. h.c., sociologist), honorary professor at the University of Geneva. Founding director (1992-2000) of the CIG; principal investigator of Swilsoo. (Christian.Lalive@socio.unige.ch)

Valérie-Anne Ryser (Ph.D. student, social psychologist), research assistant at the Interdisciplinary Institute of Life Trajectories, Faculty of Social and Political Sciences, University of Lausanne. (Valerie-Anne.Ryser@unil.ch)

Dario Spini (Ph.D., social psychologist), research assistant professor at the CIG and associate director of Swilsoo from 1998 to 2003. Since 2003, associate professor at the University of Lausanne; director of the Interdisciplinary Institute of Life Trajectories, Faculty of Social and Political Sciences, University of Lausanne. (Dario.Spini@unil.ch)

English Editing and Translation

Ian Hamilton, former chief terminologist, United Nations Office at Geneva. (Madoian.Hamilton@orange.fr)

Center for Interdisciplinary Gerontology – CIG
University of Geneva, Site de Battelle-La Villa, Route de Drize 7, CH-1227 Carouge (Genève), Switzerland. E-mail: cig@unige.ch. Web site: http://cig.unige.ch

Swilsoo's publications are to be found at: http://cig.unige.ch/recherches/swilsoo/publications.html

INDEX

A

B

C

D

G

H

M

N

O

P

Q

R

S